The
DEEP SOUTH'S OLDEST RIVALRY
AUBURN VS. GEORGIA

DOUGLAS STUTSMAN

FOREWORDS BY DAVID HOUSEL & LORAN SMITH

THE
History
PRESS

Published by The History Press
Charleston, SC
www.historypress.net

Front cover: Mark Stewart, a defensive back for the University of Georgia, breaks up a pass intended for Auburn's Tim Christian. The game took place in 1968 at Cliff Hare Stadium. *Auburn University Library Special Collections.*
Back cover, left: Tra Battle (25) leaps into the end zone after intercepting an Auburn pass. *John Kelley; right*: Cameron Newton attempts a pass against Georgia in 2010. *Morris Communications.*

First published 2017

Manufactured in the United States

ISBN 9781467137669

Library of Congress Control Number: 2017931799

Notice: The information in this book is true and complete to the best of our knowledge. It is offered without guarantee on the part of the author or The History Press. The author and The History Press disclaim all liability in connection with the use of this book.

The epitome of a rivalry is Auburn-Georgia. When Auburn and Georgia play, it's like brothers fighting. When Auburn and Alabama play, it's like in-laws fighting.
—David Housel, former Auburn University athletic director

The Florida game was big, but Auburn was always bigger. The Auburn game was the most important for us every year because it was for a championship.
—Mike Cavan, former UGA quarterback and assistant coach

That atmosphere at Sanford Stadium was the best I ever played in. Even today, I'll close my eyes and think back to 1971.
—Terry Henley, Auburn running back

The Auburn game is different. It's not like Georgia Tech and it's not like Florida. It reminds me of fighting your brother in the backyard. Even when you get through fighting, he's still your brother.
—Ray Goff, UGA quarterback and head coach

When people ask, "What was the biggest win you were ever part of?" 2002 at Auburn was the one.
—David Greene, UGA quarterback

If we had to lose, I repeat, if we had to lose, I'm glad it was Wallace Butts who beat us.
—Ralph "Shug" Jordan, following Auburn's defeat in 1959

I'm fifty-one years old, and that interception is my claim to fame. Every November, I'm dragged out of the ashes and come to life again because of that one play at Auburn.
—Steve Boswell, UGA linebacker

It's like an old neighborhood pickup game. You're friends with half the people on the other side, which makes you want to win very badly.
—Tim Christian, Auburn wide receiver and assistant coach

CONTENTS

IV. THE MOMENTS

AUBURN FOREWORD

The 1960 game against Georgia may be, arguably, of course, the most important game in Auburn history.

The importance lay not in who won the game (Auburn did, 9–6), but for where the game was played: Auburn. It was the first step toward the realization of a goal, a dream Auburn people had for more than thirty years, that of playing all of their big games in Auburn. Georgia was then, as it is now, Auburn's oldest and most traditional rival. Some say it is Auburn's most meaningful rival.

When Jeff Beard and Shug Jordan were athletes at Auburn in the late 1920s, the school's team had to play all of its big games, sometimes all of its games, on the road. That changed in 1951, when Beard became the athletic director and Jordan, formerly the line coach at Georgia, became Auburn's head football coach. They worked together to provide Auburn with facilities big enough and good enough to host all of its home games on campus.

That became reality in 1960, when Georgia came to Auburn for the first time. Actually, it had begun to change in 1959, when Jordan first took his Tigers to Athens. Auburn lost 14–13 as Georgia won Wally Butts's last SEC championship, but the Auburn-Georgia rivalry—and Auburn football—had changed forever.

It is worthy of note that of all Auburn's major rivals at the time—Tennessee, Georgia Tech, Georgia and Alabama—only Georgia, time-honored and respected foe Georgia, came to Auburn without a fight. Alabama fought the hardest, saying it would never come, but it did, in 1989. Only Georgia came freely and voluntarily, band playing, fans holding red and black banners, as if to say "We're here! Let's play!" That has not been forgotten by Auburn people.

There is a story of how the game was moved from Columbus, Georgia, where it had been played consistently for more than forty years. It wasn't an easy move.

Both schools wanted to move the rivalry game to their respective campuses, and both schools later used moving the game to justify major stadium enlargements. But Wally Butts was apprehensive, maybe a little fearful, of even broaching the subject of moving the game from Columbus. There were lots of big-time Georgia supporters in Columbus, well-heeled Coca-Cola people, who freely and generously supported the Bulldogs—as long as the Auburn game was played in Columbus. Butts was rightly afraid of incurring their wrath.

Beard and Jordan told him not to worry. They would take the heat so Butts could tell his people that he didn't want to move the game, that he fought as hard as he could to keep game in Columbus but "it's them damn Auburn people…they won't listen…they're unreasonable…don't blame me. Don't blame Georgia…blame them damn Auburn people."

It worked.

Cooperation and respect have always been hallmarks of this otherwise intense rivalry. The rivalry's history includes mutual understanding and appreciation that comes from the crossbreeding of the two coaching staffs that has taken place through the years.

Many Auburn men have gone to Georgia and won fame and acclaim, and many Georgia men have come to Auburn and done the same. Jordan, Joel Eaves, Erk Russell, Pat Dye and Vince Dooley are just five examples. There are many, many more.

The cross-pollination of coaching staffs, not just head coaches, led my friend Claude Felton, senior associate athletics director at Georgia—and the best Georgia man I know—to speculate there was an underground railroad running between Athens and Auburn. Those fortunate enough to have coached at these places were "War Dogs" or "Bull Eagles," depending on where they were coaching at the time. War Dogs were at Auburn. Bull Eagles were at Georgia.

The Georgia game was always Coach Jordan's favorite. It gave him the opportunity to see old friends, visit a stadium and a campus he cared about and respected and write another chapter in what he considered the South's greatest rivalry. Vince Dooley had similar feelings when he carried his

Georgia teams to Auburn—another example of the respect and, sometimes, even admiration that has marked this rivalry.

After Auburn's victory in the pivotal 1960 game in Auburn, Jordan said, "Maybe we should start charging ten dollars a fan to see Auburn and Georgia play." Tickets to that game were five dollars.

Looking at the price of tickets today, it is clear that Auburn and Georgia have continued to play exciting games—many, many, many of them.

Jordan studied history at Auburn, and the history of the Auburn-Georgia game always intrigued him. "After all these years," he once said, "after all the mud, the blood and the beer, Auburn and Georgia are still about even. That's probably the way it should be."

Back when I was working, Claude Felton and I would often talk about the Georgia game, or, if you prefer, the Auburn game.

We agreed that when Auburn plays Alabama and Georgia plays Georgia Tech, it's like in-laws fighting, but when Auburn and Georgia play, it's like brothers fighting.

May it ever be so.

DAVID HOUSEL

GEORGIA FOREWORD

Funny how an old story forever maintains traction.

For years, I've heard about the 1942 Auburn upset of Georgia's Rose Bowl team, 27–13, in Columbus. How Auburn's Monk Gafford was greater than Frankie Sinkwich and Charley Trippi combined that day.

The score certainly reflected the fact that Georgia didn't play like the top-ranked team in the country. This game also explains how difficult it is to go undefeated—even when you have a powerhouse team. Being a Bulldog, I have chosen to view that loss in a different way. If UGA had defeated Auburn, try to consider the embarrassment if we had lost our 1942 regular-season finale between the hedges to Georgia Tech. Might it be that Tech would have had the psychological advantage that Auburn enjoyed by facing an undefeated Georgia?

As it turned out, it was Georgia Tech that came to Athens undefeated. The winner would receive an invitation to the Rose Bowl. The Bulldogs destroyed the Yellow Jackets, 34–0, confirming the notion that there was likely a psychological significance to losing to Auburn. Subsequently, Georgia claimed a share of the 1942 national championship after defeating UCLA, 9–0, in Pasadena. You could put the Auburn upset of Georgia in this perspective when the season was over: it was like losing your girlfriend and then getting her back for keeps.

Perhaps the Auburn folks treat the 1959 Georgia-Auburn game the way Georgia partisans have always had to deal with 1942—we only talk about our victories. When a fourth-quarter fumble between the hedges allowed Georgia to recover the ball and move downfield to score a touchdown with seconds on the clock—Francis Tarkenton to Bill Herron—that '59 game became as fabled with Dog fans as the 1942 game was with Auburn aficionados.

There have been many great moments in the rivalry, the Deep South's oldest, which began in 1892. And there are undoubtedly more heroics to come.

The way the rivalry came about is one of the most fascinating college football stories of all time. Dr. Charles Herty of Georgia and Dr. George Petrie of Auburn were classmates at Johns Hopkins, where they were introduced to the game of football. When they became faculty members at their respective alma maters, they decided to organize teams and schedule a game in Atlanta for February 20, 1892.

It would be interesting if the two professors, who coached without any financial remuneration, could reflect on what has become commonplace in college football today. You know, the way coaches make millions and players get free education plus compensation. For, at the outset, it was truly an amateur exercise.

With the passing of time, the coaching staffs of each institution reflected the heritage of the other school. It began with Ralph "Shug" Jordan, an assistant for Georgia's Wallace Butts, before Auburn—his alma mater—asked him to become head coach in 1951.

Jordan took with him Buck Bradberry, Joe Connally, Homer Hobbs and Gene Lorendo—all Georgia heroes who made the transition from Red and Black to Orange and Blue and never looked back. Over the years, Georgia players became Auburn assistants and vice versa.

When Joel Eaves was hired at UGA on November 22, 1963, an amusing and funny story developed, although it was really no laughing matter. The newspapers had reported the day before that Georgia's president, O.C. Aderhold, had contacted his Auburn counterpart, Dr. Ralph B. Draughon, about the athletic director vacancy in Athens and appeared to be ready to name Eaves athletic director at UGA.

After the tragic events in Dallas, one of Eaves's neighbors was raking leaves when a friend drove by and shouted, "Did you hear they shot the President?" The neighbor, unaware of the JFK tragedy, responded, "Which one, Aderhold or Draughon?"

Eaves was miffed with the way he had been treated at Auburn, having to scout football as a secondary responsibility to serving as head basketball coach. Because of this, the opportunity to become athletic director at Georgia certainly turned his head.

Georgia folks, on the other hand, had no appreciation for hiring Eaves, a basketball coach, as its head man. They desired a well-known name with a proven track record. Adding to the anger, Eaves's first decision was to bring over Auburn's freshman coach to run Georgia's football program, which made Bulldog partisans sigh in contempt. Many UGA loyalists experienced rankled emotions and felt insulted. Quite frankly, Georgia had never experienced such depression.

Yes, Eaves hired Vince Dooley, who brought Erk Russell, Jim Pyburn, Sterling DuPree and Dick Copas—all Auburn men—with him to Athens. (DuPree had played at Auburn but had been a Butts assistant for ten years before going to Florida.)

In 1980, Dooley had the No. 1 team in the country at the end of the regular season when Auburn called to determine his interest in becoming athletic director and head coach at his alma mater. When the dust settled, he stayed in Athens, and Auburn hired Pat Dye, a one-time All American guard for the Bulldogs and a Bear Bryant protégé. Many Auburn fans were as disgruntled as Georgia alumni had been in 1963 when UGA hired Eaves, who hired Dooley. Egad! Auburn turning over its football program to a Georgia/Alabama man!

Before long, someone remembered to ask the question, "Where were Dooley and Dye on November 14, 1959?" For the record, Dye was on the field making big plays in Georgia's celebrated 14–13 victory, and Dooley was in Auburn's coaching booth.

In time, Dooley and Dye, annual adversaries in November, would retire from coaching and become men of the soil. It was not a new thing for Dye, a Blythe, Georgia farm boy, but it was for Dooley, who grew up on the waterfront in Mobile. Vince is a master gardener, historian and landscape aficionado. Pat, a radio personality in the fall, grows Japanese maples commercially. The two men have visited each other's gardens to reminisce and share notes, underscoring the notion that while the rivalry between Georgia and Auburn has been keen over the years, it has remained civil and without bitterness.

As my friend David Housel says, "It is like two brothers squaring off, fighting and roughhousing in the backyard all afternoon and then going inside and sitting for dinner."

It is interesting that Dooley became a Georgia man and Dye an Auburn man, especially with Dye's longtime affiliation with Alabama. The record shows that Dooley was the most successful coach at Georgia; Dye enjoys the same status at Auburn, which named its field for him in 2005.

There have been many times that the SEC title was on the line when the two teams played. Some of the all-time great contests for UGA occurred in 1959, 1966, 1968, 1982 and 2002. You'll find more fascinating lore about the rivalry in Doug Stutsman's thoroughly researched and well-written book.

You knew somebody had to write a book about the Deep South's Oldest Rivalry—there's simply too much history, lore and thrilling performances for it to be any other way. Doug has given us a classic insight into this ancient rivalry.

LORAN SMITH

INTRODUCTION

My first trip to Sanford Stadium, on November 18, 1991, also served as an introduction to the Deep South's Oldest Rivalry.

Both of my parents graduated from Auburn University, but at the time, my father worked under Manuel Diaz as Georgia's assistant men's tennis coach. As a second-grader living in Athens, wearing a baggy UGA Tennis sweatshirt, I watched from Section 135 as the Dogs won, 37–27. To be honest, the result didn't leave a lasting impression. What did, however, was my birthday card—or, rather, the note inscribed within it.

> *Doug,*
> *The Auburn-Georgia rivalry is different. Me and your dad went to Auburn, but Odad [my grandfather] played basketball at Georgia and he loves the Bulldogs. It's ok if you cheer for both teams because your family loves them both, too. Happy 7th Birthday, Doug. We can't wait for your first football game!*
> *Love, mom and dad*

Fast-forward twenty-six years, and times have undoubtedly changed. For the younger generation of Georgia fans, many identify 2010 (featuring Cam Newton and Nick Fairley) as the contest that escalated the rivalry into a hostile affair. A number of Auburn supporters similarly view "The Blackout" onslaught of 2007, when Knowshon Moreno and company "Soulja Boy-ed" their way to a 45–20 victory. For middle-aged alumni, memories remain from

the 1980s, when the Southeastern Conference championship was impacted by eight of ten games. Inside Auburn's Jordan-Hare Stadium, images linger from when Georgia unforgettably witnessed sugar fall from the sky in 1982. A year later in Athens, the pain of 1983 hasn't escaped Sanford Stadium after the visiting Tigers dethroned mighty Georgia.

Auburn University freshman Bo Jackson runs by UGA defender Tony Flack as head coach Pat Dye (*left*) watches from the sideline. *Morris Communication.*

In a series spanning three centuries, it's only natural for each program to feel animosity toward the other, for whatever reason. While Auburn and UGA fan bases exchange banter and insults each November, former players and coaches (as told in these pages) largely look back on their opposition with unwavering respect.

Herschel Walker went 3-0 against Auburn during his time in Athens. *Morris Communication.*

The Deep South's Oldest Rivalry began on a rainy afternoon in 1892, as thousands arrived by train and horse-drawn carriage to Atlanta's Piedmont Park. Over the next 125 years, the game has turned coaches into legends, teams into champions and players into household names. In 2011, a *Wall Street Journal* story suggested that this was the dirtiest rivalry in college football, helping prove that physical play has been a staple since the sport's inception.

Disputes between the schools date back as far as 1899, when Auburn held an 11–6 lead in the final minutes. Then, as darkness began to engulf Piedmont Park, spectators rushed the field before time expired, prompting Referee Rowbotham to call off the contest. The game was officially ruled a 0–0 tie—a decision that was protested to no avail by Auburn head coach John Heisman.

Although 1899's ending was head-scratching, the most pugilistic contest came in 1956, when Tiger defenders Jerry Wilson and Tim Baker injured Georgia quarterback Billy Hearn with a hit in the first quarter. On the next play, Ken Schulte, UGA's backup, threw an interception, and a fistfight ensued near midfield. "It was Hearn's departure which set the stage for many flare-ups the likes of which Madison Square Garden would like to book instead of that November 30 engagement between Archie Moore and Floyd Patterson," wrote Tom Kinney, sports editor of the *Columbus Ledger-Enquirer* after Auburn's 20–0 victory.

Since injuring Hearn in 1956, Auburn has experienced the "Drought of the 6s," losing to Georgia in 1966, '76, '86, '96, 2006 and 2016. And each outcome has been memorable. UGA victories in 1966 and 1976 clinched conference titles, while Auburn losses in 1986, 1996, 2006 and 2016 helped prevent the Tigers from capturing the Southeastern Conference. Yet, off the gridiron, the seemingly endless connections between two universities are what make this rivalry unique. Many family trees have links to both institutions, but none more significant than those of Vince Dooley, Erk Russell, Ralph "Shug" Jordan, Gene Lorendo, Joel Eaves and Pat Dye.

Dooley, Georgia's legendary coach, lettered in football (1950–53) and played varsity basketball (1951–52) at Auburn before kick-starting his coaching career as an assistant for the Tigers in 1956. His wife, Barbara, also graduated from Auburn. In December 1963, Dooley was hired by the University of Georgia, where he compiled a 201-77-10 record, earned six SEC titles (all clinched against Auburn) and won the 1980 national championship.

Pat Dye was born and raised on a cotton farm in Blythe, Georgia, before becoming an All-American at UGA in 1959 and 1960. After coaching stints at Alabama, East Carolina and Wyoming, Dye was hired by Auburn University, where he served as head coach from 1981 to 1992. He won four SEC titles in twelve seasons.

Joel Eaves played football, baseball and basketball at Auburn from 1933 to 1937 and was the first Tiger athlete to earn eight varsity letters. However, he's best known on the Plains as its winningest basketball coach. In 1960, Eaves led Auburn to an SEC title with a team known as the "Seven Dwarfs" because no starter exceeded six feet, three inches. Eaves conducted Auburn's hardwood program from 1949 to 1963 until being named athletic director at Georgia on November 22, 1963. His first highly scrutinized decision came on December 4, 1963, when he hired a thirty-one-year-old named Vince Dooley to be the face of UGA's football program. Eaves served as Georgia's AD from 1963 to 1979.

A Selma, Alabama native, Ralph "Shug" Jordan played football, basketball and baseball for the Tigers between 1928 and 1932 and received his first coaching position at Auburn. After Jordan returned from World War II in 1945 (he received a Purple Heart), recently hired Auburn coach Carl Voyles expressed displeasure over assistant coaches

Malcolm Mitchell celebrates after scoring a touchdown in 2014 at Sanford Stadium. *Morris Communication.*

being allowed to join his staff after the war. Disheartened by Voyles, Jordan left Auburn and was hired by the University of Georgia in 1946. He headed UGA's basketball program and was also an assistant football coach on Wallace Butts's staff. Jordan coached in Athens through 1950, when he was urged to return home by Auburn athletic director and college friend Jeff Beard. Jordan applied for the coaching vacancy by writing a letter that stated, "I hereby apply for the position of head football coach at Auburn. If you don't believe in Auburn people, you ought to close the place down." Jordan coached Auburn from 1951 to 1975.

When Jordan was chosen by Auburn in 1951, he brought along Gene Lorendo, who had played football and basketball at Georgia from 1946 to 1949. Lorendo (a star hoopster for Jordan at UGA) remained as an offensive assistant at Auburn for each of Jordan's twenty-five seasons.

Erk Russell (Georgia's helmet-butting defensive coordinator from 1964 to 1980) attended Auburn from 1946 to 1949, lettering in football, baseball, basketball and men's tennis. After his playing career, Russell was an assistant football coach and head baseball coach at his alma mater before being hired by Dooley at UGA in 1964. Russell served as Georgia's defensive coordinator for four SEC titles and the 1980 national championship.

"It's almost like a brother-sister rivalry," said David Greene, UGA quarterback from 2001 to 2004. "My dad, granddad and sister all went to Auburn. My brother-in-law, Matt Clark, kicked for Auburn. The

connections between the schools are endless and the fact we play so late every season makes it unbelievably special."

For 125 years, the contest has sparked headlines across southern newspapers, applauding some of the greatest college football games ever played.

1941: The Augusta Chronicle: Sinky Pass Sinks Auburn
1965: The Atlanta Journal: Bryan Returns to Haunt Dooley
1971: The Birmingham News: Sullivan's Bombs Win Biggest Game Ever for Jordan's Tigers
1994: The Birmingham News: AU Streak Dawg Gone
2007: The Atlanta Journal-Constitution: Black Magic

The series began in Atlanta, made brief appearances in Macon, Montgomery, Athens and Savannah, and then turned to Columbus, Georgia, for home in 1916. For four decades, the teams battled in a crammed Memorial Stadium, a mere 36 miles from Auburn and 174 miles from Athens. It was here where the game became, well, a rivalry. After 1958, the series bid farewell to Columbus and implemented a home-and-home agreement that stands today.

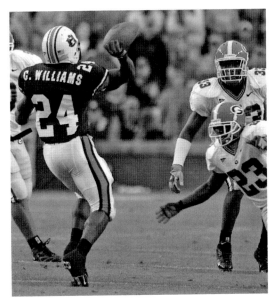

Cadillac Williams completes a touchdown pass during Auburn's 24–6 win over UGA in 2004. *Morris Communication.*

"I have many great friends who are Auburn Tigers," UGA historian Loran Smith said. "We get along 364 days a year—all but that one Saturday every November."

Georgia leads the all-time series 57-55-8.

I

THE BEGINNING

A sellout crowd is shown at the 1942 Auburn-Georgia game at Memorial Stadium. *Auburn University Library Special Collection.*

I
MEMORIAL STADIUM

A Home Found in Columbus: 1916 to 1958

Most fans know the Auburn-Georgia rivalry by two venues: Sanford Stadium and Jordan-Hare Stadium. For decades, however, that wasn't the case. In 1916, with approval from school administrators, Columbus, Georgia, won the right to host the game, outbidding the likes of Macon, Montgomery and Birmingham.

With prominent alumni from both schools calling Columbus home, the town put on a show like few others in 1916. Parades, parties and pep rallies lasted days, prompting the *Columbus Ledger* to print on the morning before kickoff, "Columbus, the manufacturing center of Georgia and the cotton mill center of the south, has changed to a college town."

When both teams arrived, they were welcomed by notable graduates. Former UGA quarterback George "Kid" Woodruff met Georgia at the Waverly Hotel. A delegation of alumni did the same for Auburn, greeting the Tigers at the Ralston Hotel. Columbus believed it had one chance to impress both universities, and the town didn't disappoint. As the morning of the 1916 game arrived, a train from Auburn pulled into Columbus carrying more than one thousand students, a billy goat, Auburn's brass band and four thousand yards of orange and blue ribbon. Notable politicians from each state attended, as did school presidents, chancellors, professors and former team captains. Simply stated, it was a who's who of Auburn and Georgia.

But as thrilling as the week of activities were, the 1916 contest matched in excitement. Scoreless after three quarters, Auburn kicker Moon Ducote kicked a 45-yard field goal off teammate Legare Hairston's leather helmet to secure the 3–0 victory. The maneuver prompted a rule change that stated the ball must be kicked directly off the ground. After the game, the *Atlanta Constitution* boasted, "Ducote was the star of the most hectic football struggle believed to have been played in the south this season."

Prior to 1916, Columbus had won the right to host the game for only a year, but following the performance the city delivered, an extended contract was verbally agreed to on the night of Auburn's victory. School directors finalized a multiyear contract on October 1, 1919.

1920

Although the Deep South's Oldest Rivalry was held thirty-nine times in Columbus, only once did the matchup feature a pair of unbeaten teams. In 1920, Auburn, coached by Mike Donahue, arrived with a 5-0 record, having outscored opponents 206–8. Georgia (4-0), led by first-year head coach Herman J. Stegeman, had bested its opposition 111–3. However, when the high-powered offenses met on October 30, 1920, the game turned into a defensive struggle. Georgia had never beaten Auburn in Columbus, but that changed in front of a raucous standing room only crowd of around eight thousand. UGA won, 7–0, en route to its first unbeaten season (8-0-1) since going 4-0 in 1896.

Following the game, O.B. Keeler of the *Atlanta Journal* wrote, "It was the first victory of the Red and Black over the Plainsmen since the heroic days of the McWhorter era and it probably was the biggest upset on the Georgia side in the long and eventful history of the two elevens."

However, seemingly every time the game was played in Columbus, the city stole the show. In a *Columbus Ledger* column by John Buford Brock, the journalist stated, "For twelve months the city has been waiting in anticipation of this annual classic; for two months they have made preparations and for the last two days the city has gone as mad as a March hare."

After upsetting Auburn (man-for-man the heavier team), UGA supporters held impromptu parades throughout Columbus, capped by a late-night dance at Haleyan Hall. Oddly enough, Auburn students were invited to attend the function, and the two schools partied into the night. The *Columbus Ledger* claimed, "The most interesting feature of an Auburn-Georgia game is the splendid friendly relations between the two colleges. If Auburn had to lose a game of football, no worthier victor would be picked than the Red and Black team."

NOT SO FRIENDLY: 1956

Thirty-six years after students rejoiced in unison, their football teams had no intention of playing peacefully in 1956. Entering the contest, Auburn was favored by two touchdowns, while UGA had sustained key injuries throughout the season—mainly to receivers Roy Wilkins and Jimmy Orr.

Plainly put, Georgia arrived at Memorial Stadium with a 3-4-1 record and beat up. It left with a 3-5-1 record and knocked out. Late in the first quarter, Auburn defenders Jerry Wilson and Tim Baker tackled Georgia quarterback Billy Hearn, causing the signal-caller and star baseball pitcher

Auburn lineman Tim Baker holds a photo of the 1956 fight at Memorial Stadium. *Tim Baker family.*

to separate his shoulder. On the ensuing play, backup Ken Schulte heaved a pass toward the end zone that was intercepted by Jimmy Cook at Auburn's five-yard-line. As Cook came down with the ball, a full-fledged fistfight was happening near the original line of scrimmage. Georgia lineman Harold Deen Cook and Baker initiated the blows.

Baker spoke about the incident in March 2016:

> *I have a big photograph of the fight framed in my home, but here's what happened: The play before the fight, Georgia went back to pass and I got by [their offensive line]. Well, when I got to Georgia's halfback, he blocked me but Cook didn't like the fact I got by him first. So the next play, Georgia started a fight with me and, you know, I fought back. Right then, Georgia's halfback got into it too and that's when everything broke loose.*

Both benches stormed the field, as did coaches, police officers and a handful of sideline spectators. The brawl lasted until Auburn's band was instructed to play "The Star-Spangled Banner." With national pride at an all-time high in the 1950s, both squads stopped throwing punches and returned to their benches—all in respect for their country. Furman Bisher, sports editor of the *Atlanta Constitution*, wrote, "Severely disguised but not quite lost in the pugilistic process was a 20–0 football victory the Tigers scored before a packed house of 26,000 fans, often as wild, delirious and fanatical as the conflict of gladiators down on the earthen floor before them."

After the first-quarter melee, there was peace until the third quarter. With Auburn ahead 20–0, four players—two from each side—were penalized for inciting more skirmishes. The third-quarter fight ended with flags on UGA tackle Riley Gunnels and halfback Gene Littleton, while Auburn end Jerry Sansom was also punished. Auburn evened the number of penalties in the fourth quarter when tackle Jeff Weekley was flagged.

According to Gunnels, the third-quarter ruckus began when Auburn back Bobby Hoppe was seen kicking Littleton. Gunnels was flagged for his retaliation. Following the incident, Gunnels's father—who played at UGA in the 1930s—charged toward Georgia's sideline from his seat at Memorial Stadium.

"My dad almost went on the field," said Gunnels, who played professionally for the Philadelphia Eagles. "I'll never forget, though, he came and stood right beside me near our bench."

The memorable 1956 contest marked the sixtieth playing of the Deep South's Oldest Rivalry, and it remains the most violent.

MEMORIAL STADIUM

The thrill of playing host never dwindled for Columbus. In 1942, the *Athens Banner-Herald* wrote a half-page article laying out festivities that awaited students when they arrived: barbecues, costume parties, parades and elegant balls. During the tenure of head coach Wallace Butts (who was hired in 1939), the Georgia team would often drive to Lions Municipal Golf Course and hold a Friday workout on the fairway of hole No. 12.

On game days, however, it was all about Memorial Stadium. The iconic football arena was opened in 1925 and named in memory of World War I veterans from Columbus. "They called Memorial Stadium a neutral site but there wasn't anything neutral about it," said Nat Dye, Georgia lineman from 1956 to 1958 and older brother of Pat Dye. "There were always more Auburn fans."

With the venue 36 miles from Auburn and 174 from Athens, the number of supporters did typically favor the Tigers. In 1955, Auburn fans roared during their 16–13 victory, often mocking UGA with chants of, "Bow Wow, Bulldog, Bow Wow—Erp, Erp!" The "Erp's" meant to simulate a crying puppy. Georgia fans returned the banter with yells of, "We've got Auburn worried." Auburn countered with, "We've got Wally worried!"

Although the size of Memorial Stadium was far from ideal, the game remained in Columbus in large part because of notable alumni who called

Georgia head coach Wallace Butts said of the decision to move the game from Memorial Stadium, "It's like losing a member of your family." *UGA Athletic Department.*

the city home. Frank Foley, whose name is christened on UGA's baseball field, practiced law in Columbus. George Woodruff, for whom UGA's practice fields are named, became a successful businessman in the city. Then there were Art Lynch and Alfred Young, Georgia and Auburn alumni, respectively, who many felt fought hardest to keep the contest in Columbus through their ties in the community. Both died in 1953 within months of each other, and in their honor, the Lynch-Young Memorial Trophy was created in 1954 and given annually to the game's Most Valuable Player. It was presented from 1954 until the game left town in 1958. It hasn't been awarded since.

On the day of the 1953 contest, Latimer Watson wrote in the *Columbus Ledger*: "It's Christmas and Fourth of July and New Year's Eve all rolled into one. It's the day when Columbus puts aside its city ways, its dignity, and for an all too short time, becomes a rollicking college town."

Two years earlier, a pregame incident in 1951 left Georgia coaches irate about the conditions at Memorial Stadium. According to the *Columbus Ledger-Enquirer*, dressing rooms had a coal-burning heater and toilets were hooked up to the same water line as the showers.

In 1951, Auburn athletic director Jeff Beard entered the locker room and noticed steam coming from the toilets each time they were flushed. "I fixed our side but Coach Butts didn't notice it on the Georgia side," said Beard, who died in 1995.

Prior to kickoff, UGA star John Carson flushed and was burned by the scorching water. "Naturally, [Butts] thought it was from us," Beard said. "I remember him saying, 'Those Auburn people would do anything to win.' He was so mad we didn't know if he was going to play the game or not."

The thrills, however, did eventually end. Following the 1958 game, Auburn and Georgia left Columbus and moved the game to respective campuses. At the time, none of Auburn's four rivals (UGA, Georgia Tech, Tennessee and Alabama) would play at Cliff Hare Stadium, in part because of the facility's limited capacity. Auburn would embark to Neyland Stadium (Tennessee) and Grant Field (Georgia Tech) in odd-numbered years, but both schools played Auburn at Birmingham's Legion Field in even-numbered years. The Auburn-Alabama game was also annually held at Legion Field. It wasn't until 1970 that Georgia Tech came to Cliff Hare Stadium. Tennessee didn't play at Auburn until 1974. On December 2, 1989, Alabama arrived.

So, with a limited number of home games in the late 1950s, Auburn jumped at the opportunity to leave Columbus. On January 16, 1959, school officials announced that the contest would no longer be played at Memorial Stadium. The move left Columbus bitter and heartbroken. The following morning, UGA athletic board member Bradley Driver Sr. told reporters, "The University of Georgia and Coach Butts did everything possible to keep the game in Columbus. The pressure to move came from Auburn."

Bob Pruitt, sports editor of the *Columbus Enquirer*, wrote a scathing column on January 17, 1959:

> *Moving the game was a low blow to the people of this area who, during the lean years, had supported it wholeheartedly. Not too many years ago, Auburn's football appeal was weaker than skimmed milk and one could buy a ticket to a game played in Auburn easier than buying a postage stamp. Although denied by most college officials, moving the game from Columbus proves without a doubt that college football is big business and not just a college sport.*

In all, the matchup was held thirty-nine times at Columbus venues, still more than at Sanford Stadium (thirty games through 2016) and Jordan-Hare Stadium (twenty-nine through 2016). From 1916 to 1958, the only time the game wasn't played in Columbus was 1929, when Athens hosted to honor the opening season of Sanford Stadium. In the Columbus meetings, Georgia won twenty-one times, Auburn won sixteen and the teams twice played to a tie (1937 and 1949). World wars canceled games in 1917, 1918 and 1943.

In 1959, when asked about the decision to leave Memorial Stadium, a somber Wally Butts said, "It's like losing a member of your family."

2

GAME 1

FEBRUARY 20, 1892, AUBURN 10, GEORGIA 0

Ten steps into Auburn Arena, a silver cup, or trophy if you will, sits enshrined in glass casing. The memento acts as the starting point of a history tour through Auburn athletics, eventually leading to displays for Charles Barkley, men's swimming and diving, Bo Jackson and the 2010 national championship football team. However, before any modern

UGA's inaugural football team in 1892. *UGA Athletic Department.*

accomplishment, there's a shrine to history professor Dr. George Petrie—or, as Auburn calls him, "our most important recruit ever."

Petrie is known as the patriarch of Tigers football for introducing the sport to the Agricultural and Mechanical College of Alabama, now known as Auburn University, after witnessing the activity while studying at Johns Hopkins in the late 1800s. Also at Johns Hopkins was Dr. Charles Herty, a chemistry professor for the University of Georgia. During their time in Maryland, the educators agreed to bring football back to Auburn and Athens, and they vowed to compete against each other. Petrie coached Auburn's first team; Herty coached Georgia's.

Petrie and Herty arranged the inaugural game of the rivalry for February 20, 1892, which turned out to be a rain-soaked, muddy afternoon at Atlanta's Piedmont Park. Petrie got the best of his friend, earning Auburn's first win, a 10–0 upset victory. In honor of the achievement, Auburn players were presented a silver cup that includes the following inscription:

> *Prize for intercollegiate football contest*
> *Georgia Alabama*
> *Won by A&M College Auburn, Ala.*
> *Atlanta, GA*
> *Feb. 20, 1892*

More than a century later, the prize—now stained and slightly rusted—remains a fixture in history, greeting fans at the front of Auburn Arena.

As for the game itself, conditions were far from ideal, prompting Petrie to say afterward, "Not often, if ever, have I been as happy as I was when that game was over." According to the *Atlanta Journal*, around three thousand people arrived by train, carriage, buggy and horseback for the afternoon kickoff. Because Georgia Tech had yet to field a football team, students from the Atlanta school showed up wearing UGA colors as a form of state pride. An *Atlanta Journal* reporter, assigned to write about sights and sounds, mentioned Georgia Tech's contingency: "One hundred and fifty students from the technological school are on their way to the grounds on foot. Every one of them wears the crimson and black of Athens. They are carrying cowbells."

Touchdowns counted for four points, and a goal was two points. Auburn scored all ten of the game's points in the second half.

AT THE UNIVERSITY OF GEORGIA, the 1892 contest isn't remembered for the final score. Rather, the school's proudest moment occurred hours before kickoff on the train ride from Athens to Atlanta. According to Thomas Walter Reed, a University of Georgia historian who attended the game, so many Athens residents wanted to support their school that a train was chartered by Southern Railway.

"As I remember, there were five passenger coaches and they were packed to the doors with students and citizens," Reed wrote in his 1945 book *History of the University of Georgia*. "The coaches were elaborately decorated in red and black and the locomotive was adorned from the pilot to the tender."

Throughout the train ride, fans shouted the Georgia yell:

Hoo-rah-rah! Hoo-rah-rah!
Hoo-rah-rah! Georgia!

Upon reaching the town of Lula, a small, discreet railroad junction between Atlanta and Athens, the conductor had to wait for another train to pass. During this time, Reed taught him how to play the Georgia yell on the locomotive.

Toot-toot-toot! Toot-toot-toot!
Toot-toot-toot! Toooot!

"Lula is sixty-six miles from Atlanta, and that engineer blew the Georgia yell at least five times for each mile," Reed wrote.

Passengers begged the engineer to continue playing Georgia's yell into Atlanta, but an ordinance prohibited the blowing of locomotives within city limits. Upon hearing this news, Reed wired Atlanta's mayor and close friend, the Honorable William A. Hemphill, and requested permission to keep the tune going. "I received his favorable answer at Norcross and the engineer, with great pride, kept that whistle going right up to our stop," Reed wrote. "The people of Atlanta must have thought the world was coming to an end."

There was no bulldog mascot at the game, but rather a goat named Sir William that wore ribbons down his horns and a black coat with red "U.G." on each side. Prior to the game against Auburn, Sir William (owned by student Bob Gantt) looked on as UGA defeated Mercer University, 50–0, to claim its first victory in school history.

"Georgia was quite confident going into Auburn because of beating Mercer," said Vince Dooley, UGA head coach from 1964 to 1988. "So after Auburn pulled off the victory, Georgia students didn't take too kindly to losing."

In a story Dooley often retells, Georgia's mascot suffered the biggest defeat of all. "Georgia students and alumni were so depressed that they decided to barbecue the goat," said Dooley, laughing. "It was the first postgame tailgate. And, you know, that was the end of the goat. Beat Mercer, lost to Auburn."

PETRIE WASN'T PAID FOR COACHING Auburn's first football team. In fact, he had to borrow money to make the sport a reality.

As for the 1892 contest against Georgia, the railroad ran a special train from Montgomery to Atlanta, which consisted of an engine and two coaches.

Students from Montgomery's Starke University occupied one coach, and Auburn players and students were in the other.

According to Petrie, he had been invited to watch UGA practice while on a business trip to Athens and admitted, "I thought they would run roughshod over us." Georgia students felt confident, too, as many took torches to Atlanta with hopes of holding a torchlight parade after winning. In the end, touchdowns by Rufus T. Dorsey and J.L. Culver gave Auburn an unlikely triumph.

Petrie later told reporters, "The celebration was not staged, but would have been if Auburn had located Georgia's torches."

ADDING HISTORY TO THE FIRST CONTEST, one legend claims the 1892 game is where Auburn's battle cry "War Eagle" originated. According to the Auburn University Athletic Department, it's the most popular tale about the creation of the famous saying. It's also categorically false.

The article was published in 1960 by student Jim Phillips, then editor of the school newspaper, the *Auburn Plainsman*. Phillips wrote that three young men from Alabama—Cal, William and Eugene—went to fight in the Civil War and took part in the Battle of Appomattox Court House. In Phillips's myth, Cal and William succumbed to their injuries while Eugene lay unconscious on the Virginia battlefield. When Eugene woke, he heard crying from a wounded eagle named Anvre and nursed the bird back to health. The two later returned to Auburn, where Eugene became a popular professor of history. Phillips wrote that Eugene would often bring Anvre to his classes in Broun Hall and the eagle became loved by students.

Eugene and Anvre attended Auburn's inaugural football contest, the tale continued, against UGA. After a scoreless first half, Auburn took the lead, at which point Anvre left Eugene and began circling the field. As the game neared its conclusion, Anvre—who was about thirty years old at the time—toppled and died at Piedmont Park. Following the game, the bird was buried by Auburn's team captain, who said during the burial: "Anvre was a real war eagle. The rest of the season we'll win for him and 'War Eagle' will henceforth be our personal battle cry."

Just like that, "War Eagle" was born. So, too, was the Deep South's Oldest Rivalry.

II
THE COACHES

3
PAT DYE

Tucked away on 940 acres of land, Pat Dye spends most days wearing duck boots and Carhartt pants. In his mid-seventies, his days of coaching have come and gone. His days of planting, however, are in full force this pristine day near Auburn University's campus.

It's 8:28 a.m. on September 10, 2015, and Dye has been up since 4:30. Most days, he eats breakfast before sunrise and then labors on his land until nightfall. He raises trees, grows plants and cares for horses and donkeys.

"I haven't shot a gun in five years," Dye said as he climbed into his golf cart. "Things I loved most as a child, they don't bring me joy anymore."

Dye was born in 1939 on a farm in Blythe, Georgia, and more than seven decades later, land and football are two loves that remain unscathed.

DRIVING AROUND HIS PROPERTY, Dye's mind traveled many places over three and a half hours, to distant times and distant memories. But when talking about his football career, he didn't start with earning All-American honors at Georgia or winning four Southeastern Conference titles while coaching Auburn. He began with December 2, 1955, in the visitors' locker room of

Opposite, top: UGA head coach Vince Dooley is carried off the field following a 31–21 victory over Auburn in 1980. *The* Augusta Chronicle.

Opposite, bottom: Pat Dye shakes hands with UGA coach Ray Goff after beating the Bulldogs 20–3 in 1989. *Morris Communication.*

LaGrange High School. On that day, the junior at Richmond Academy in Augusta, Georgia, had just experienced the toughest defeat of his young career. With a spot in the Class AA state championship on the line, Richmond Academy lost 20–13 to LaGrange, which scored all its points in the opening half.

"It still haunts me," said Dye, shaking his head. "We had no business losing to LaGrange."

The final score wasn't all that ate at Dye. In the locker room after the game, as tears stained his cheeks, the seventeen-year-old saw a group of seniors who he didn't believe were taking the loss hard enough. "That's when I called my junior teammates together," Dye recalled. "I said, 'Y'all come here. We're gonna be right back next year with the same opportunity…and we ain't losing.'"

However, unexpected changes were looming at the Augusta military school. That offseason, Richmond Academy coach Harry Milligan left for Darlington School, prompting assistant Frank Inman to be promoted to head coach. The news shocked Dye, whose older brothers, Wayne Jr. and Nat, had also played for Milligan. Inman's tutelage, however, became a key piece in Pat Dye's puzzle of learning what it takes to win.

Inman, a Duke University graduate, hired two assistants, Major Tallent and Fred McManus, and the three coaches joined forces to establish what Dye calls "the toughest football team I ever played for."

It didn't take long for Dye to embrace Tallent, his position coach. Tallent, a former Arkansas guard, had a plate implanted in his mouth after getting hit by Doak Walker in a game against Southern Methodist. He had coon dogs and would often take Dye and teammate Tommy Ashe on late-night hunts. In all his years playing football, Dye says no individual coach was better than Tallent. Still, it was the combination of personalities between Inman, Tallent and McManus that took Richmond Academy to unexpected heights.

"Coach Inman was very smart—taught chemistry," Dye said. "But at times you'd think he was sadistic. Coach McManus, well, you knew he was. There was no question about McManus. And then you had Coach Tallent. Coach Tallent was on the fringe."

Throughout 1956, it became clear that Dye's senior class wasn't littered with overpowering ability. They lost to North Augusta and Camden Academy while tying Boys Catholic, 0–0, in the final game of the regular season. With a 7-2-1 record, Richmond Academy limped into the 1956 state playoffs as two-touchdown underdogs to Lanier High (Macon). But after

Pat Dye helped the Academy of Richmond County win the 1956 state championship.
Morris Communication.

scoring fourteen points in the opening three minutes, the Augusta team held tight for a 14–7 victory. Waiting for Richmond Academy in the state championship game was unbeaten Northside High (Atlanta) and All-State quarterback Stan Gann, who had outscored opponents 355 to 45.

On the day of the game, a torrential downpour hit Augusta, postponing the contest to Saturday and equalizing the playing field. Forced to compete in sloppy conditions, the flashy Atlantans sputtered, and Dye's underdogs stunned the state.

"We barely noticed that ankle-deep mud," Dye said of the 13–7 victory. "Coach Inman had our team so dang tough we could've played in a salt mine."

According to teammates, a key to victory was Dye's discovery while watching game film the morning before kickoff. "Pat got to school early and began watching tape on Northside," high school teammate Charles Moody said. "He noticed an alignment pattern for when they planned to run right and when they planned to run left. Pat had Northside figured out before we took the field."

In the locker room after the game, Dye again wept—this time tears of joy—while McManus handed out celebratory cigars. McManus had become a father the morning of the game, and Richmond Academy players weren't sure if the stogies were for parenthood or the state championship. Either way, Dye, who's not a smoker, lit the gift and exited the locker room. Waiting outside was University of Georgia head coach Wallace Butts.

"I walked out with my cigar lit and it dang near took Coach Butts' breath away," Dye said. "He didn't know what to say or how to say it. When I saw his expression, I thought, 'Damn, I guess I've done something really wrong here.'"

Eight days later, Dye signed with UGA.

ALL THREE DYE BOYS ENDED up at UGA, but it wasn't easy. Growing up around twenty miles south of Richmond Academy, the task of getting to school tested Wayne Jr., Nat and Pat. The three would often hitchhike to class, catching rides on Highway 1 from morning travelers or milk delivery trucks.

"Getting to school was the easy part," said Nat, the middle boy. "Getting home was the problem."

With practice often dragging to nightfall, the Dye boys spent countless nights with teammates or, in Pat's case, at the home of local banker Tom Nichols. The Nichols family owned a community bank in Blythe and lived on Milledge Road, just blocks from Richmond Academy. According to *Augusta Chronicle* archives, when Pat was in junior high, he made a promise to

Pat Dye (60) stands with older brother Nat Dye during their playing days at UGA. *UGA Athletic Department.*

the family. "I don't have any money to pay you for letting me stay here," Pat told Tom Nichols. "But about eight years from now, you can tell people an All-American slept in that bed."

About eight years later, Dye proved true to his word, earning 1959 All-American honors as a guard for the University of Georgia. The story helps summarize the childhood of Dye, who was always confident. Not cocky, but confident. Like the time he turned five and received his first new pair of shoes. There was a couch in the Dyes' living room where his father would stretch after long hours in the Georgia heat. But when Wayne Sr. came home that night, he found Pat in his spot, grinning ear-to-ear, making sure his daddy saw those sneakers.

To the delight of Wayne Sr., all three of his boys earned football scholarships from Coach Butts: Wayne Jr. (1953–56), Nat (1955–58) and Pat (1957–60).

While the youngest Dye took each game seriously, there was always one opponent he saved his best for: Georgia Tech. Throughout his senior year at Richmond Academy, Dye was heavily recruited by the Yellow Jackets and one day received a guarantee from the man recruiting him.

"You have to be careful when you tell people what they can't do," Dye said. "People will fool you. In 1956, Georgia hadn't beaten Tech in eight years and the coach recruiting me goes, 'If you go to Georgia, you'll never beat Georgia Tech.' You know, I never did forget that. As a coach and player, my record is 12–0 against Georgia Tech."

Dye's streak began in 1957 in the annual Thanksgiving Day freshman game between the Bullpups and Baby Jackets. The contest, benefiting the Scottish Rite Children's Hospital, became a nationally recognized event showcasing many future All-Americans from both schools. It's safe to say, however, that no athlete was ever more fired up for a freshman game than Dye.

As UGA prepared for its opening kickoff, Dye was positioned as the farthest man near Georgia Tech's sideline. Bill Force, who played with Dye at Richmond Academy, competed for Georgia Tech and was watching near Tech's bench.

"I'm standing with my teammate, Lloyd Sutter, and I say, 'Lloyd, there's Pat Dye—we won a state championship together in high school,'" Force recalled. "Well, Lloyd looks at Pat and Pat's crying. I mean tears were coming out like a waterfall. Lloyd goes, 'Your boy's crying! What in the world is wrong with him? He's sobbing!' I said, 'That's right. And we're about to get our ass kicked.'"

The Bullpups won, 13–7, beginning Dye's personal dominance over Georgia Tech. Two of Dye's greatest games at Georgia came against the Yellow Jackets: during his junior season in 1959, when Georgia beat Georgia Tech, 21–14, and in 1960, his senior season, when Georgia won, 7–6.

Dye laughs when it's brought up, but older brother Wayne Jr. (who died in 2007) claimed that Pat was never emotionally ready unless he shed tears before a game. In 1959, Dye's parents and two older brothers drove to Athens the morning of the Georgia Tech contest and waited for team buses to arrive. Nat had just finished his first season in the Canadian Football

League and hadn't seen his younger brother in nearly six months. As buses pulled up, Wayne Sr., Nell and Wayne Jr. hid in front of Nat as Pat walked toward his family.

"When Nat stepped in front of us, Pat just busted out," Wayne Sr. told the *Augusta Chronicle* in 1959. "Wayne [Jr.] said 'He's ready today,' and I guess he was. Pat told us Sunday he thought that was the best game he'd ever played."

Dye might have edged his 1959 performance against the Yellow Jackets in 1960. In the final game of his Georgia career, Dye blocked a field goal and an extra point to help secure that 7–6 victory at Sanford Stadium. Despite being an All-American guard, Butts positioned Dye at defensive end for the extra point, and he blocked the kick with his face. After the victory, Dye kept a game ball for his efforts.

Although his dominance over Tech was personally satisfying, UGA's greatest team accomplishment came during Dye's junior season in 1959. Entering '59, Georgia hadn't posted a winning record in five years, and most preseason polls picked UGA to finish eighth in a ten-team league. But thanks in part to the play of a junior guard, the Bulldogs rallied to a 10-1 record and emerged as unlikely SEC champions. The title-clinching contest came on November 14, 1959, when Georgia snapped a six-game losing streak to Auburn, handing the Tigers a 14–13 defeat in Athens.

Looking back on 1959, Dye admits there was more talent on Georgia's 1958 team. But as he had learned during his junior year at Richmond Academy, talent doesn't always lead to championships. "We should've won ten games in 1958," said Dye, as memories flooded back. "But we were so splintered as a team.

"That first game against Texas—lost 13–8. Should've won.

"Lost to Vandy by seven—should've won.

"Lost to Florida, 7–6—should've won.

"Got beat by Alabama when they had less than one hundred yards of total offense. We had more than four hundred and got beat, 12–0."

Following the 1958 season, UGA linebacker David Lloyd turned professional, leading critics to believe his departure would doom the Bulldogs. Instead, after Lloyd was taken in the fourth round of the NFL draft, Georgia's 1959 team became inseparable. "We really came together after Dave went pro," Dye said.

The same tight games that hindered UGA in 1958 were won by the Bulldogs in 1959: 17–3 over Alabama; 21–6 over Vanderbilt; 21–10 over Florida.

No cigars were smoked after securing the SEC against Auburn, and five years after leaving Athens, Pat Dye redirected his focus into becoming *Coach Dye*.

DYE BEGAN HIS COACHING CAREER in 1965 as the linebacker coach under Paul "Bear" Bryant at the University of Alabama. Bryant tutored his disciple for nine years before Dye became head coach at East Carolina University (1974–79) and at the University of Wyoming (1980). Then, on November 30, 1980, Dye received a call from Don Leebern that forever changed his life. Dye and Leebern were linemen together at Georgia, and the two had remained close in the ensuing decades—years that saw Leebern become one of the country's most powerful boosters.

"The Sunday after Georgia beat Georgia Tech, I get a call from Don," recalled Dye, looking back on November 1980. "He asked, 'Do you wanna be the head coach at Georgia?' I said, 'What are you talking about?' Don said, 'Vince [Dooley] is going to Auburn.'"

Added Leebern: "Pat's up in Laramie, Wyoming, and I say, 'Pat, is it cold up there?' Pat said, 'Don, listen. It's a dry cold—like dry-ice cold. If I look out my back porch I can see all the way to Canada.'"

Georgia was a month away from playing Notre Dame for the 1980 national championship, while Dye had led Wyoming to a 6-5 record. To put it mildly, the call shocked Dye. "I told Don, 'Hell yeah, I'd love to coach Georgia,'" Dye remembered. "Now I don't think I would've gotten it. Look, I know Don's strong and maybe he would've been strong enough; but I don't know if he would've been strong enough to keep Erk Russell from getting it."

Leebern said: "My first choice was Pat Dye. There's no question about that. Pat would've been coming home and he would've brought great enthusiasm to Athens. He knew the state. He knew recruiting. I wholeheartedly believe Pat would have been a great fit in Athens."

In the end, we'll never know. Two days later, Leebern again reached out to Dye with different news. "Tuesday morning Don calls back and says, 'Pat, Vince is staying at Georgia but you ought to try and get the Auburn job,'" Dye said.

Leebern told Dye to call Fob James, the governor of Alabama, and provided a number to the governor's office. That afternoon, Dye had James—who had been a star football player in the 1950s at Auburn—on the other line.

"I said, 'Mr. Governor, what about your coaching job over there?'" Dye asked. "Fob James said, 'Pat, I'm out of the loop. I was involved before but I ain't involved in this.'"

Before hanging up, however, James instructed Dye to call Auburn University president Hanley Funderburk, who was meeting with a search

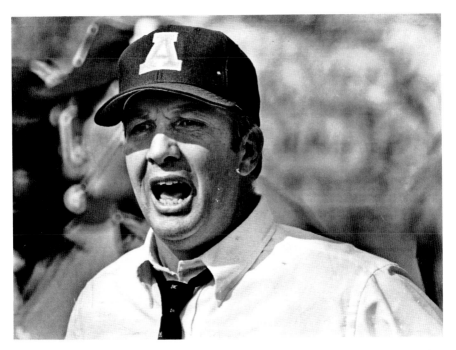

Pat Dye coached at Auburn for twelve seasons and led the Tigers to four SEC titles. *Morris Communications.*

committee. To Dye's pleasure, the committee had already put his name on a list of candidates, marking the start of one of the most hectic months of Dye's life. With Dye now interested in Auburn, Wyoming wanted answers, and when its first-year coach was unable to provide them, Wyoming's athletic department gave him an ultimatum.

"Wyoming told me I had three options," Dye recalled. "Sign a contract with them. Resign. Or they'd fire me."

After meeting with Wyoming officials, Dye went home and asked his wife, Sue, to hand over a yellow pad. Refusing to get fired, Dye wrote: "In the best interest of the University of Wyoming football program and my coaching career, I hereby resign as the head football coach of Wyoming."

At forty-one years of age, Dye was unemployed and without a clue if Auburn would offer him a position. After remaining in Laramie for about ten days, Dye grew tired of being on the wrong end of sidewalk stares. "I'll tell you one thing, when I walked up and down the streets of Laramie after resigning, they'd look at you a little sideways," Dye said. "So I went back to the house and said, 'Sue, let's get out of Laramie.' We went to Steamboat Springs and snow-skied for a week while Auburn figured things out."

After a month of considering the likes of Dick Sheridan, Bobby Bowden, Jackie Sherrill, Grant Teaff, Dan Reeves and Billy Adkins, Auburn selected Dye to lead its program. Even now, Dye isn't sure how he earned the position, other than having two important supporters in his corner.

"I think they hired me because Dr. Funderburk and Bobby Lowder [founder of Colonial Bank and long-serving trustee at Auburn] liked me," Dye said. "Bobby wasn't on the committee but the committee couldn't hire a coach without his approval. He paid half the salary through personal services. Also, Bobby was the only one who did due diligence on me. He checked my background all the way from high school, through college, through service. He checked my coaching background at Alabama, East Carolina and Wyoming. The whole deal. Bobby said, 'This is the guy we need to hire.'"

When Bobby Lowder spoke, Auburn's administration often listened. So, on January 2, 1981, Dye signed a $100,000 contract to coach the Tigers, immediately turning a University of Georgia family into Auburn fans. For older brother Nat, switching allegiances was a no-brainer.

"When your brother's fighting on the street corner, what are you gonna do?" asked Nat, before quickly answering. "You have his back every damn time. Every damn time."

For Nat's children, however, becoming Auburn supporters overnight wasn't easy for classmates to understand, especially while living in Georgia. "It was hardest on my children," Nat admitted. "I sat my kids down and said, 'Y'all are gonna pull harder than anyone for your uncle.'"

Auburn University head coach Pat Dye signals to his team before facing Georgia in 1992. *Morris Communication.*

Pat Dye patrolled Auburn's sideline from 1981 to 1992, leading the Tigers to four SEC championships and a 1983 Sugar Bowl victory. From 1969 to 1980, the twelve years prior to Dye's tenure, Auburn went 3-9 against Alabama. During Dye's tenure, the Tide and Tigers were 6-6.

"If you're going to have success at Auburn, you have

to be on even terms with Georgia and Alabama," Dye said. "I was .500 against Alabama and 7-5 against Georgia. The only team I didn't have a winning record against was Florida."

Dye paused again, gently stepping out of his golf cart. Suddenly, his mind raced back to defeats that shouldn't have been. "We lost two games in Gainesville that were terrible, terrible losses," he said.

For 1983 Auburn quarterback Randy Campbell, Dye's legacy on the Plains goes far deeper than his twelve seasons as head coach. In Campbell's mind, Dye set the tone for decades to come. From the SEC's inception to Dye being hired in 1981, Auburn won one conference title (1957). From 1981 to 2015, Auburn won seven, ranking only behind Alabama and Florida. "Auburn had been good in the past but never consistently a top program until Coach Dye was hired," Campbell said. "Coach Dye deserves so much credit for turning Auburn into what it's become."

Auburn SEC titles before Dye: 1957
Auburn SEC titles since hiring Dye: 1983, 1987, 1988, 1989, 2004
(coached by Tommy Tuberville), 2010 (coached by Gene Chizik) and
2013 (coached by Gus Malzahn)

Dye's tenure as head coach ended in 1992 following an NCAA investigation that revealed booster Corky Frost made illegal payments to Auburn defensive back Eric Ramsey. As football coach and athletic director, Dye was accused of lacking institutional control but was not found to have any knowledge of the payments. In the wake of the investigation, Dye stepped away following the 1992 season.

Still, after leaving the sidelines, Dye's legacy remained strong. Everlasting, in fact. On November 11, 1994, Dye was named Head Football Coach Emeritus by Auburn president William Muse, joining Ralph "Shug" Jordan as the only coaches to receive the honor. During the presentation, Auburn athletic director David Housel handed Dye a piece of the Berlin Wall as a symbolic gesture of Dye getting rival Alabama to travel to Jordan-Hare Stadium for the first time in 1989. When Alabama came to Auburn, Dye compared the moment to Germany tearing down its dividing barrier.

On November 19, 2005, the grass at Jordan-Hare Stadium became known as Pat Dye Field. Nine years later, Dye was enshrined in the University of Georgia "Circle of Honor."

IN ATHENS, DYE'S NAME HAS BEEN a topic of conversation long after his final game in uniform. His most memorable—and controversial—moment came four games into the 2002 season, when he boldly stated on a Birmingham radio show that Georgia wasn't "man enough" to beat Alabama. Dye was confident the comment would ruffle feathers. He also believed it was true.

"I knew my words would set a fire under Georgia," Dye said. "But at the time Georgia hadn't shown what they showed that day at Alabama. They didn't look all that great against Clemson or South Carolina."

After making the comments, Dye called UGA offensive coordinator Neil Calloway (Dye's assistant for twelve seasons at Auburn) and UGA defensive line coach Rodney Garner (who played for Dye at Auburn). "I told Neil and Rodney, 'I've done my part,'" Dye said. "'Now y'all go do yours.'"

> Added Calloway: "Our offensive linemen were very mad—they asked why he would say that. I told them, 'After we win the game, we'll call and ask.' And that's exactly what we did."

Georgia answered Dye's criticism after receiving a punt with 3:45 remaining in the fourth quarter. Trailing 25–24, UGA called six straight running plays, setting up kicker Billy Bennett for the game-winning score. Final: Georgia 27, Alabama 25. Not long after the game, Dye's phone rang with UGA's offensive line on the other end.

"The call came from Neil, but they passed that phone to every player on the bus," Dye said. "It tickled me to death."

The victory in Tuscaloosa helped propel Georgia to the 2002 SEC championship—its first since 1982.

"When I first made that 'man enough' comment, everyone in Athens hated me," Dye said. "In the end, everyone in Tuscaloosa hated me."

More than ten years after the Georgia-Alabama game, *Athens Banner-Herald* reporter Marc Weiszer wrote a column on September 10, 2013, after the University of Georgia announced its 2014 Circle of Honor recipients. The article's opening sentence read, "Pat Dye is *man enough* to be inducted into Georgia's Circle of Honor."

EVEN THOUGH PAT DYE WANTED his alma mater to beat Alabama in 2002, it's Auburn that has his heart today. After Sue and Pat divorced in 1998, Pat moved to his hunting preserve, two turns off Wire Road and about ten miles from Auburn University's campus. He still has his own radio show and does segments for eight additional stations. He also does advertising and speaking appearances.

"The combination of them all," Dye said. "That's what keeps this wheel rolling."

The wheel is his land. Dye spends countless hours planting trees, improving his nursery and cleaning the garden. There's always another project—the latest is building an area near his pond where he hopes people will come and get married. In addition to plants, Dye has redirected his love for hunting animals to raising them. Not far from his nursery are two horses, Cam and Bo.

"They pull the wagon," said Dye as he went underneath a fence to greet them. "Bo, he'll let you pet him all day. Cam? Well, Cam's a little more elusive."

After spending time with Cam and Bo, Dye walked to the next fence where two donkeys, Ollie and Polly, were awaiting attention. His animals love him, nesting their heads on Dye's chest each time the former coach goes near a fence. But as much as animals fascinate him, it's trees Dye can't get enough of. For Dye, each specimen is like a former player, needing a place for its roots to expand. Dye doesn't want two large trees too close together. He also doesn't underestimate the importance of making each weather its own storm.

"To have a healthy specimen, you have to let it stand on its own two feet," Dye said. "If he's growing right under another tree, and isn't withstanding the elements, he'll always be a runt. Last thing you want is a bunch of runts."

WHEN DYE LEAVES HIS LAND, it's usually to drive to Auburn. Since arriving on campus on January 2, 1981, it's hard for him to put the changes he's witnessed into words. New academic buildings. New athletic arenas. New bars and restaurants. But as Auburn University has progressed structurally, the school's environment has changed in ways that remind Dye of a different campus he fell in love with.

"Auburn today is what Georgia used to be," he said. "Look, there are a lot of kids at Georgia who would fit in great at Auburn, but there aren't a lot of Auburn students who would fit in at Georgia. At Auburn, you don't have to be somebody before you get here to be somebody when you get here. That make sense? It doesn't matter if you drive a pickup or Mercedes. Don't care if you're from Mountain Brook, Buckhead or Aliceville. Your social status doesn't matter at Auburn. All that matters is that you chose Auburn."

Dye said goodbye to Ollie and Polly and reentered his golf cart. It was almost 11:30 a.m., and he was meeting friends for lunch at noon. Inside his office, his secretary, Lynn Huggins, marked two photographs for Dye to sign for a fan named Sarah. The coach personalized each, finishing by writing "War Eagle." He then climbed into his pickup.

In fifteen minutes, he'll be in Auburn.

4
VINCE DOOLEY

Vincent!" said Barbara Dooley, kindly shouting up the stairs in their Milledge Circle home. "Doug's here for your interview."

Wearing a white T-shirt and Georgia shorts, Vince Dooley appeared from the corner, grabbed half a chocolate donut and sat in what he calls "My Bulldog room."

"This is the first donut I've had in ten years," Dooley said in October 2015. "It's actually very good."

About a mile away, his life-size statue towers over the corner of South Lumpkin and Pinecrest Drive. But it's 392 miles from Athens, in Mobile, Alabama, where Dooley's journey began. Raised by two parents whose education didn't exceed grammar school, Dooley was the first in his family to attend college. His sister Rosella was the first to graduate high school. "My father was a chief electrician," Dooley said. "Mother a housewife. And while they had no formal education, they had great morals. You know, that's probably more important than an education."

Dooley attended McGill Institute, where he excelled in football and basketball and hoped to focus on the latter. However, once senior basketball season began, football recruiters refused to let him play in peace. One night after practice, Dooley was attempting to get dinner when representatives from the University of Alabama insisted a collegiate decision be made.

"There was an Alabama coach in the front seat and another one in the back," Dooley recalled. "That turned me off to Alabama. When I got home, I ran up the stairs and called Auburn. I was ready to commit."

THE EARLY YEARS

In September 1950, Dooley enrolled at Auburn, where he played both football and basketball. Joel Eaves was an assistant football coach while also heading the basketball program. Early in his freshman year, Dooley established a relationship with his basketball coach, both men unaware of the lasting effect it would eventually have on the University of Georgia.

Then, there was football. As a member of Auburn's freshman team, Dooley—a quarterback—watched from afar as the varsity team went 0-10. Auburn lost to Wofford College. And Southeastern Louisiana. And Tulane. The Tigers were shut out seven times, marking the end of coach Earl Brown's tenure on the Plains.

"My freshman team didn't even associate with the varsity," Dooley said. "They were so undisciplined and uncommitted."

During the offseason, Auburn graduate Ralph "Shug" Jordan was hired from the University of Georgia, where he had spent four years as an assistant football and head basketball coach. Jordan brought with him UGA alumni Gene Lorendo, Homer Hobbs and Buck Bradberry while keeping Auburn alumnus Joel Eaves on staff. The crew immediately elevated Auburn's football program to a 5-5 record in 1951. However, with high expectations in 1952, Dooley injured his knee twice, and Auburn went 2-8. As Dooley was recovering, he attempted to play for Eaves when a third knee injury occurred.

Vince Dooley, while serving as Auburn's freshman coach in the early 1960s, is pictured with Tiger players Tucker Frederickson (30) and Jimmy Sidle (12). *Auburn University Library Special Collections.*

"The doctor said, 'I'll get you ready for football season but when you get to be forty you'll have a bad knee,'" said Dooley, pointing toward a scar. "Well, when you're twenty you don't even think about turning forty."

Dooley had surgery and was named team captain as a senior in 1953. Healthy again, the quarterback led Auburn to a 7-3-1 mark (the program's best record since 1936), including a 39–18 victory in the Deep South's Oldest Rivalry. Dooley's 1953 win marked the first time Auburn beat UGA since 1942.

Entering the 1953 game at Memorial Stadium, Jordan used two offensive units, coined "X" and "Y." The X squad started each contest, was quarterbacked by Dooley and featured five seniors, two juniors and four sophomores. The Y outfit was guided by quarterback Bobby Freeman and had five sophomores, five juniors and one senior. On November 14, 1953, the combination of Dooley and Freeman proved unstoppable for Georgia's defense. In front of a record crowd of twenty-six thousand patrons (including Major John Eisenhower, son of President Eisenhower, and famed World War II general Omar Bradley), Dooley led Team X to three touchdowns and a convincing twenty-one-point win.

After the Auburn victory, Tiger fans paraded through Columbus, many shouting, "We can quit talking about 1942!" Even the scoreboard operator—an Auburn graduate—promised to keep the 39–18 result visible at Memorial Stadium until kickoff the following year. Dooley's victory over UGA propelled Auburn to a school record six straight wins over the Bulldogs from 1953 to 1958.

After the 1953 season, Dooley earned an invitation to the College All-Star Game in Chicago, marking the end of his collegiate career. The morning of his graduation, the quarterback was commissioned as a second lieutenant in the Marine Corps, for which he served from 1954 to 1956. Following service, Dooley had to decide his future.

"There was an offer for me to stay in the Marine Corps," he said. "I thought hard about that. I also thought about entering the banking business in Mobile. I was very fortunate to have a few options, including one from my former coach, Shug Jordan." In the end, Dooley accepted a position on Jordan's coaching staff—beginning his career on July 16, 1956.

The twenty-three-year-old was hired for an annual salary of $5,100.

PERSONNEL FORM NO. 2

RECOMMENDATION FOR APPOINTMENT
The Alabama Polytechnic Institute
Auburn, Alabama

Date Prepared __July 16, 1956__

TO THE PRESIDENT:

The following recommendation is submitted for your consideration:

__Vincent J. Dooley__

Name   Local Address

To the position of (Official Title) __Assistant Football Coach__

To be paid at the rate of $ __5,100.00__ per annum on a 12 mos. **X** Full time **X** basis

9 mos. _____ Part time _____
(If part time state what percentage)

From __Auxiliary Enterprises__ FUND __Auburn Ath. Dept.__ Department $ __5,100.00__

From _____ FUND _____ Department $ _____

From _____ FUND _____ Department $ _____

From _____ FUND _____ Department $ _____

This recommendation is for:

1. ( ) Appointment of Additional employee
(Explanation of addition, if not budgeted, to be attached as well as two copies of record of Applicant — Personnel Form No. 1)

2. (**X**) Appointment to position formerly held by __Charlie Waller__
__Resignation__
(State if vacancy is due to retirement, leave, or resignation, etc.)

3. ( ) Advance in salary from $ _____ to $ _____ per annum.

4. ( ) Change in rank or title from _____ to _____

5. ( ) Reinstatement from Leave of Absence or inactive Status.

6. ( ) Change in funds as set out above.

7. ( ) Transfer from _____ to _____

APPOINTMENT, REAPPOINTMENT OR CHANGE OF STATUS TO BECOME EFFECTIVE AS OF
__August 25, 1956__ .
(date)

Additional Information: _____

Approved:

Ralph B. Draughon

President

JUL 20 1956

Date _____

Head of Department

Dean or Director

Submit in quintuplicate.

Vince Dooley's first contract as an assistant coach at Auburn University. *Auburn University Library Special Collections.*

DOOLEY AND JOEL EAVES

After Dooley returned from the Marine Corps, Jordan assigned him as an assistant in Auburn's scouting department, where Eaves was the head scout. For five years, Dooley and Eaves left the Plains on Friday and traveled to watch Auburn's future opponent. Dooley would pack a projector, and the two would study film in their hotel room.

Their work together was lauded, as Auburn won the 1957 national championship, and Dooley's paycheck increased to $6,300 by June 11, 1958. Eventually, Dooley was promoted to main scout and later head coach of Auburn's freshman team. Eaves also earned a promotion—but not from Auburn. In November 1963, Eaves was named athletic director at the University of Georgia and was immediately tasked to find a football coach to replace Johnny Griffith, who was fired by UGA after the '63 season.

"Coach Eaves was in a dilemma," Dooley recalled. "Georgia was going through all these problems and he couldn't bring himself to recommend a freshman coach from a rival school."

The men stayed in touch, and eventually Eaves asked Dooley if he'd be willing to come to Georgia as an assistant. However, Eaves was unaware that Dooley had plans of his own. After being at Auburn twelve years (four as a player, eight as coach), Dooley was ready to embark on a new adventure. The thirty-one-year-old planned to leave the Plains and become an assistant under Frank Broyles at Arkansas or under Darrell Royal at Texas. Then, when Coach Jordan left Auburn, Dooley's dream was to return and lead his alma mater. As talks with Broyles developed, the Arkansas coach called looking for Dooley, but when Dooley couldn't be found, Broyles reached out to Eaves to help locate Auburn's freshman coach.

"I believe that's what put Coach Eaves over the top," Dooley said. "That was the nudge he needed to hire me. After offering me the job, Coach Eaves said, 'By the way, Frank Broyles called and he wants you to be an assistant coach. Now what do you want to be, an assistant coach or head coach?'"

On December 4, 1963, Dooley and his twenty-three-year-old wife, Barbara, moved to Athens on a frigid night to rejuvenate a once thriving program in Athens.

THE CONTRACT

To put it mildly, the hiring of Dooley wasn't overly popular on the streets of Athens. "Only three people believed it was a good hire," Dooley said. "Coach Eaves, myself and my wife."

Dooley signed a $15,500 contract ($12,000 base salary and $3,500 in incentives), while the contract remains framed beside his back door on Milledge Circle. For Dooley, money wasn't a concern. After all, it was $6,080 more than he was making at Auburn. But before agreeing, he pushed Eaves to extend the length of his deal.

"Coach Eaves wanted to give me three years and I begged for four," Dooley said. "Getting a four-year contract was very important because I needed to tell recruits, 'When you come to Georgia, I'll be here till you leave.'"

Eaves reluctantly gave in, and the Dooleys moved into a furnished apartment for a portion of 1964 before renting a home for $150 a month on Milledge Circle—the same property they live in today.

UGA defensive coordinator Erk Russell gets his head rubbed by Vince Dooley. *The Augusta Chronicle.*

As important as finding a home was, it was also crucial to assemble a quality coaching staff, and Dooley began by targeting Auburn alumni. He hired his former teammate, Jim Pyburn, a baseball and football standout at Auburn in the early 1950s. Pyburn coached defensive line, linebackers and secondary under Dooley from 1964 to 1979. Next, Dooley and Eaves convinced Sterling DuPree, the lead recruiter at the University of Florida, to leave Gainesville for Athens. Dupree, who was a former assistant at UGA under Wallace Butts, had been a two-sport letterman at Auburn and once finished third in the NCAA 100-yard dash behind Jesse Owens and Ralph Metcalfe. When asked in 1964 about his decision to leave Florida, Dupree said, "I have a great deal of attachment for Georgia. My daughter went there and I love those turnip greens."

Dooley and Eaves also hired Dick Copas, a 1960 graduate of Auburn University, to become Georgia's head trainer. At the time Copas was working at Furman University, but had gotten to know Dooley and Eaves as a student trainer on the Plains.

"Dooley was an assistant coach and I was a student trainer under the great Kenny Howard," Copas said. "We all used to travel together."

Copas worked in numerous capacities at UGA from 1964 to 1996, and during games, he served as Dooley's *get back* coach. According to Copas, when players moved too close to the field, it was his job to get them back.

"We'd been in Athens about [three years] and the SEC got concerned about people being run over on the sideline," Copas said. "It became my job to make sure that didn't happen."

In 1971, Eaves approached Copas and asked if he'd fill in for ten days as Georgia's golf coach while they searched for a replacement for Howell Hollis. Turns out, Copas was the ideal fit, eventually leading the Bulldogs from 1971 to 1996 and winning seven SEC titles. In 2006, Copas was nominated to Georgia's Circle of Honor, where Dooley had been enshrined two years earlier.

"I owe a lot to Coach Dooley and Coach Eaves," Copas said. "Coach Dooley is a great man with a wonderful family. And let me say this: He belongs in the Circle of Honor. When they gave me the award, I was totally unprepared for that. I told Coach Dooley, 'I don't deserve this.'"

In addition to adding Pyburn, Dupree and Copas, Dooley, not long after being hired by Georgia, received a call from a fourth Auburn alumnus: Erk Russell. "When I got to Georgia, Erk called me," Dooley remembered. "In his typical way, Erk goes, 'Hey, Vince, how 'bout a job?'"

TURNING GEORGIA AROUND

It didn't take long for Dooley's Dogs to start winning. After UGA combined for seven victories in 1962 and 1963, Dooley matched that win total in his inaugural campaign in 1964. Dooley again posted a winning record in 1965 and began catching the eye of other teams. Following the 1965 season, Dooley received a call from former Oklahoma Sooners coach Bud Wilkinson, whom Dooley admittedly admired.

"Coach Wilkinson called and said, 'Oklahoma would like to hire you,'" Dooley remembered.

Dooley flew to Oklahoma and met with school officials. After getting off the plane, he was greeted by media members, and the idea of Georgia's coach leaving for Norman, Oklahoma, began to worry Eaves. After all, Dooley had shaped UGA into an emerging national power with upset victories in 1965 over defending national champion Alabama and in Ann Arbor versus Michigan.

"There was a real outcry for me to stay, and Coach Eaves made my financial package a little better," Dooley said. "But I decided to stay because I had just gotten started."

The ordeal with Oklahoma not only frightened loyalists in Athens, it also proved to be a lesson-learner for the young coach. Throughout the next fifteen years (1966–80), Dooley made sure his name wasn't associated with coaching vacancies. Did he receive offers? Sure. Did he entertain them? Not until November 1980.

"I didn't think it was good to have your name out there every year," he said. "So after 1965, I never considered another school until Auburn—my alma mater."

Although Dooley's first two seasons in Athens were deemed a success, there was one team he couldn't topple: Auburn. In 1964, during Dooley's first matchup with Coach Jordan, Auburn senior Tucker Frederickson stole the show, rushing for 101 yards to spark Auburn's 14–7 triumph. According to Frederickson, three years earlier, in 1961, Dooley was head coach of Auburn's freshman team when the Tigers faced Alabama.

During the heated battle, Auburn's staff designed a kickoff formation where blockers were supposed to lead Frederickson up the right sideline.

"Our whole team was blocking right, but I ran left and scored a touchdown," said Frederickson, the first overall pick of the 1965 NFL draft.

Fast-forward three years, and Frederickson was now returning kickoffs *against* Dooley. With both teams struggling to score, Auburn again designed a formation where Frederickson was supposed to follow blockers up the right sideline. However, similar to 1961, the Heisman Trophy finalist returned Georgia's kickoff and darted left.

Forty-two yards later, he was taken out-of-bounds near the Bulldogs bench.

"I was tackled right next to Coach Dooley," Frederickson recalled. "Vince said, 'Damn, I remember you did that as a freshman. I should've told our guys.'"

After losing another heartbreaker to Auburn in 1965, Dooley beat the Tigers for the first time in 1966 and was crowned SEC co-champions with Alabama. The victory came on Auburn's home field, where Dooley clinched five of his six SEC titles. The 1966 team brought hardware to Athens for the first time since 1959, and a book, *Georgia Bulldogs 1966*, was published to honor the championship squad. Inside the pages, Dooley's oldest daughter, five-year-old Deanna, wrote a chapter titled "My Daddy Is Not a Football Coach."

> *Everybody calls my daddy Coach Dooley, but I just call him Daddy. He's a nice man. He rests. He takes me to the dime store. He plays tennis. He goes on trips. Some things he does I don't know about. He does everything.*
>
> *Mama says I shouldn't marry a football coach, 'cause all they do is play football and never come home.*

Following the historic 1966 campaign, Georgia again won the SEC at Auburn in '68. And again at Auburn in '76. And again at Auburn in '80. Finally, during the 1980 season, Fob James, who was serving as governor of Alabama, reached out to Dooley and pitched the idea of becoming head coach and athletic director at Auburn.

"With Fob James and the emotional pull," said Dooley, before collecting his thoughts. "You know, of course Barbara was interested in returning to Auburn because that's where she went to school, as well."

"I thought we were going," Barbara added. "But neither of us ever regretted the decision to stay."

Although Georgia was 11-0 and a month from playing Notre Dame for the national title, rumors swirled through both states that Dooley had accepted the position. The gossip even reached members of the 1980 Bulldogs team. Hugh Nall, Georgia's center, was hunting with teammate Scott Woerner in Thomaston, Georgia, when they heard the news.

"We walked in after deer hunting and mom goes, 'Well, y'all lost your coach to Auburn,'" Nall recalled.

Vince Dooley won six SEC titles during his twenty-five-year reign as Georgia's head coach. *The* Augusta Chronicle.

Emotions swirled in Athens, as feelings of confusion, anger and resentment entered the locker room. "The seniors were very disappointed with the timing of the announcement," Frank Ros, captain of Georgia's 1980 team, wrote in an e-mail. "We had worked so hard to get to where we were. We had bought into 'big team, little me,' and we were at the pinnacle of our journey when it popped up."

In late November, Vince and Barbara were ready to fly to Auburn for a meeting when they picked up their youngest child, Derek, from ball practice. Upon hearing his dad's opportunity, the twelve-year-old made his opinion clear. "Derek was in the backseat and started crying," Vince recalled. "He said, 'I hate Auburn. I ain't going to Auburn.'"

Vince and Barbara still boarded the plane, but images of their crying son never left. Adding clarity to the decision, when Vince returned from Auburn, he walked into his home and began looking around the walls. After seventeen years in Athens, UGA memorabilia covered Milledge Circle with photos of every All-Conference player and team captain he ever coached.

"My roots at Georgia had become deeper than my roots at Auburn," Dooley said. "I'd been here seventeen years, and when Derek did that, it made me think about my children. They didn't know Auburn like Barbara and I knew Auburn. All four grew up Georgia."

Dooley informed Governor James that he planned to remain in Athens, where a month later he won the school's first Associated Press national championship. Auburn, with a recommendation from Dooley, hired former UGA All-American Pat Dye. Looking back on Auburn's offer, Dooley says it was all about timing.

"If I had been at Georgia five, six, maybe eight years, I would've jumped the Chattahoochee to go back to Auburn," Dooley said. "But I thought about my family and all those players. I told myself, 'I've been here too long.'"

Still, after informing Auburn he wasn't coming, the coach had to face his team. Knowing rumors had reached the locker room, Dooley requested a meeting with the 1980 senior class. His question was simple.

"Coach Dooley asked if we'd take him back," Ros recalled. "We all said 'yes.'"

After deciding to stay, Dooley's program went on its most dominating stretch in school history, compiling a record of 43-4-1 from 1980 to 1983, including three SEC titles, the 1980 national championship and a Heisman Trophy winner (Herschel Walker, 1982).

THE AUBURN-GEORGIA RIVALRY

In twenty-five seasons at UGA, Dooley went 11-13-1 against Auburn: 6-6 against Ralph Jordan; 2-2-1 against Doug Barfield; and 3-5 against Pat Dye. Dooley may have clinched all six of his conference titles against Auburn, but his alma mater also prevented him from winning SEC championships in 1971, 1978, 1979, 1983, 1987 and 1988. Still, despite having endless fond memories about the rivalry, when Dooley was asked about his favorite contest, his mind raced in another direction.

"Right away, the disappointing ones come to mind," he said. "The first one I think back on is that two-point loss in 1965. The toughest was probably '71—we were both undefeated and we helped Pat Sullivan win the Heisman Trophy. Then there was '83, when we had gone four years without losing a conference game before that night in Athens."

Dooley gently tapped his coffee table as he reached for a drink. After taking a sip of tea, the negative thoughts disappeared. "You know, we upset

Auburn a lot when it looked like they were headed to the Sugar Bowl," he said. "That was a big-time win in 1970. Oh, and of course '86."

Throughout the years, Dooley was able to put aside his connection to Auburn, simply viewing the Tigers as another opponent. In a quarter century, only once did the moment prove too big: 1975. It was the final time Jordan and Dooley would face each other, and after defeating his mentor in Athens, decades of memories were triggered during the postgame handshake.

"It all flashed back," Dooley said. "Walking to midfield I thought about playing for him, him giving me a chance to coach and then all our years competing."

Standing on the Sanford Stadium grass, a handshake wasn't enough on November 15, 1975.

"I embraced him," Dooley said. "I had to embrace him."

III

TOP 10 GAMES

Pat Sullivan (7) runs off
the field during the fourth
quarter of Auburn's 1971
victory at Sanford Stadium.
*Auburn University Library
Special Collections.*

5

NO. 1. THE UNSUNG HERO

NOVEMBER 13, 1971, AUBURN 35, GEORGIA 20

On Georgia's first two extra points, I could feel air go past my fingertips. I was
that close to blocking them. On the third try, I got it.
                                                    —*Roger Mitchell*

The idea for this book was sparked by an off-the-cuff comment from legendary University of Georgia swim coach Jack Bauerle. For my twenty-seventh birthday, Bauerle offered me a pair of tickets to the 2011 Auburn-Georgia game with an agreement I would take his middle son, Magill. Deal. So ten months after Auburn had won the national championship, I walked with the Bauerles toward Sanford Stadium.

"All I've heard this week are fans wanting revenge for what happened last year with Nick Fairley," Coach Bauerle said. "You know, fans say a lot of things, but the only Auburn loss that still hurts happened right here forty years ago. I'll never forget 1971."

Bauerle briefly went quiet as we walked through Gate 8. Then, as if the game was yesterday, he uttered nine words: "How the hell did he block that extra point?"

Magill and I looked at each other, both clueless about 1971. At that point, I realized research needed to be done. And research led to finding Roger Mitchell.

8-0 vs. 9-0

On November 13, 1971, a crowd of 62,891 people flooded Sanford Stadium, the largest at the time in UGA history. Thousands more stood on rooftops and train tracks, fighting for a glimpse of one of the most anticipated games ever played in the South. On display were two undefeated programs: Auburn (8-0) and Georgia (9-0) with the loser eliminated from SEC title contention. It was the first time since 1920 that both teams met without a loss—and it hasn't happened since. Still, decades later, it's not the undefeated records that remain in the mind of Auburn reserve cornerback Roger Mitchell.

"It was the atmosphere," Mitchell said. "Most frenzied atmosphere I was ever part of."

The excitement in Athens was one neither team had ever witnessed, while scenes remain with Auburn players forty-six years later. Hundreds of fans slept near the stadium on Friday night to claim their spots on the railroad trestle. The hill outside Sanford Stadium was covered with spectators more than three and a half hours before kickoff.

"I was sitting on our bench next to backup quarterback Dave Lyon," Mitchell said. "Dave leaned over, and in his Lowndes County accent said, 'Rog, can you believe all these people? It looks like a million pigeons up there.'"

Auburn running back Terry Henley said: "I get chills down my spine just thinking about that atmosphere. More than four decades later, people still come up and say, 'I was there. I remember that moment in Athens.'"

Auburn, deemed a slight underdog by odds makers, arrived a day before kickoff and immediately went to Sanford Stadium. Waiting anxiously were thousands of Georgia fans holding signs and banners, chanting at Auburn quarterback Pat Sullivan. Georgia had a defensive back named Phil Sullivan, and throughout practice, fans taunted Auburn with chants of, "Sullivan to Sullivan." As Georgia fans continued to yell, Pat Sullivan approached teammate Dick Schmalz. "Pat came up and he was so excited," Schmalz recalled. "He walked past me and said, 'Dick, we're gonna do it.'"

Auburn completed its walkthrough and went to check-in at its hotel, the Holiday Inn in downtown Athens. Throughout the night, Georgia fans ran wild on hotel breezeways, doing their best to keep Auburn awake.

"Those frat boys kept me up all night," said Mitchell, laughing. "They were ringing bells, beating on doors, running on the rooftop. But I tell you what, all that did was fire us up even more."

Ralph "Shug" Jordan (*left*) shakes hands with Vince Dooley after Auburn beat Dooley's Dogs in Athens in 1971. *Auburn University Library Special Collections.*

Added Schmalz: "We stayed adjacent to Georgia fraternity houses and students somehow found a way to get from the roof of a fraternity house to the rooftop of our hotel. It was absolutely crazy."

Adding to the scene, when Auburn arrived at Sanford Stadium the next day, fans surrounded both team buses and began rocking the vehicles. Inside, Auburn stayed quiet.

"I was on Coach [Shug] Jordan's bus and none of us said a word," Mitchell remembered. "Then, I'll never forget, Coach Jordan stood up and said, 'If any of you get out of line, you won't dress for this game. You better act like gentlemen. Then, after you do that, we'll show them how to play football.'"

THE GAME

Roger Mitchell isn't mentioned on the official stat sheet from November 13, 1971. In fact, the walk-on from Eufaula, Alabama, wasn't even listed on press box rosters. Prominently documented were Pat Sullivan's 248 passing yards and four touchdowns—two to Terry Beasley and two to Schmalz. Sparked by Sullivan, Beasley and Schmalz, Auburn raced out to a 14–0 advantage before Georgia quarterback Andy Johnson steadily marched the Bulldogs back. With Auburn clinging to a 21–14 fourth quarter lead, Johnson scored to pull Georgia within one point. Then, Mitchell pulled off what he calls "the play that gave me a name."

First, before discounting a blocked extra point as luck, it's important to understand the relationship between Mitchell and blocking kicks. For Mitchell, it had nothing to do with luck. It was a skill. Better yet, it was his art. At 155 pounds, Mitchell wasn't offered a scholarship from Auburn out of high school, so he enlisted in the U.S. Coast Guard Academy with hopes of gaining 15 pounds. The strategy proved successful, and Mitchell transferred to Auburn as a walk-on with enough size to compete in the Southeastern Conference. However, as a transfer, he was forced to sit out 1970 and was immediately placed on the scout team.

"I played every scout team position there ever was," Mitchell said. "1970 was brutal, but there was one good rule about scout team: If you blocked a kick, you got to go in early. So you better believe I blocked one every day. I blocked punts, blocked field goals. It became my specialty."

Mitchell's reputation was quickly recognized, and Jordan made him a special-teams starter in 1971. Mitchell took so much pride in his position that, before games, he would track down a sideline referee and explain quirks he had noticed about an opponent's field goal unit. "I'd start politicking before every game," Mitchell said. "I told the official in Athens that Georgia's center had a little rock before he snapped, which he did, and I was going the instant he started rocking. Sometimes they'd listen, sometimes they didn't."

In Athens, Mitchell's politicking paid dividends. As Georgia attempted to tie the game at 21, Mitchell darted off the left edge and blocked the extra point.

"When Andy Johnson scored, Georgia was roaring back like a house on fire," Henley said. "It was the loudest I've ever heard a stadium in my life. But I tell you what, Roger Mitchell turned the hose on them. Roger Mitchell single-handedly put out that fire."

On Auburn's first play after receiving the kickoff, Sullivan connected with Beasley, who bounced off two defenders and ran seventy yards to the end

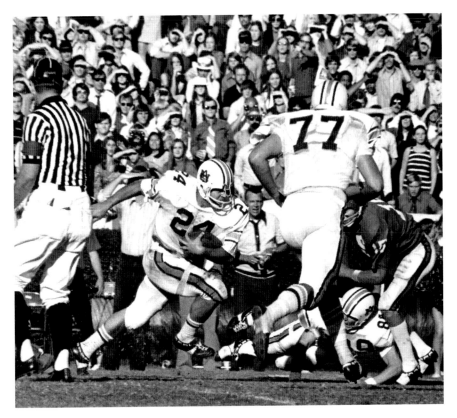

Tommy Lowry carries the ball against UGA in 1971. *Auburn University Library Special Collections.*

zone. In a span of fifteen seconds, what might have been 21–21 was now 28–20. The Tigers tacked on another score and prevailed, 35–20.

"That victory was the best moment of my career at Auburn," Schmalz said. "To be part of that team, in that atmosphere, with that result—wow."

After the game, Auburn players ripped away Georgia's famed hedges, while Coach Jordan was presented a piece of greenery in the locker room. Jordan told reporters, "Mrs. Jordan has a brass candelabra at home and I think it will look very nice there."

FOR DICK SCHMALZ, AS IMPRESSIVE as his individual stat line was, he's quick to admit he was also competing for Sullivan's opportunity to win the Heisman Trophy. In 1971, voters submitted their ballots following the Auburn-Georgia game, and the Tigers understood that a sharp performance by their quarterback would likely clinch the coveted award.

"Riding home, we didn't talk about beating Georgia as much as we did Pat's chance of winning the Heisman," Schmalz said. "Look, its Pat's trophy. It'll always be his trophy. But Pat made sure we all felt responsible for him winning it."

Sullivan's performance in Athens helped him narrowly edge Cornell back Ed Marinaro for the 1971 Heisman Trophy, the first in Auburn history. Sullivan said of the honor, "This is the second greatest thing that's ever happened to me. The first is playing football for Coach Jordan and Auburn."

After beating Georgia, the Tigers lost its final two games in 1971, falling to Alabama for the SEC title and to Oklahoma in the Sugar Bowl. UGA finished with wins over Georgia Tech and North Carolina, but its defeat to Auburn cost the Bulldogs a chance for a national title. Years later, the loss hasn't been forgotten by head coach Vince Dooley.

"I had two orthopedic surgeons, Mixon Robinson and Chuck Heard, hanging all over Sullivan that afternoon," Dooley recalled. "Pat still threw four touchdowns to beat us. Looking back, there was actually too much excitement on campus that week. I think we would have been better off playing at Auburn because we were too excited. Our team was ready to play on Tuesday."

TWO THINGS WERE NEVER THE SAME following Auburn's 1971 victory in Athens: a Javelin patrol car owned by the Alabama Department of Public Safety, and Tommy Yearout's back.

Let's start with the state vehicle that escorted Auburn's team to Athens. The individuals responsible remain a mystery, but as Auburn attempted to sleep at the Holiday Inn, they awoke Saturday to find a beat-up police car in the parking lot.

"Those students broke almost every light on that thing," said Henley, laughing at the memory. "I remember riding home and it looked like our police car had been in a demolition derby. That only added to the atmosphere."

Mitchell said: "Oh man, they tore up our police escort. I mean, they tore it up. That poor car had no idea what it had comin' when it got to Athens."

The second battering occurred to Yearout's back. With Pat Sullivan garnering most of the attention in 1971, the play of Auburn's defense was largely overshadowed, including the consistency of All-SEC tackle Tommy Yearout. Yearout, a Birmingham native, was the defensive captain, but he often felt as though his efforts weren't fully appreciated.

"Understand this," Yearout said. "Pat Sullivan is my dear friend but our defense received very little publicity in 1971 because of him. Look, we were trying to get a Heisman Trophy winner at Auburn because before Pat there had only been three Heisman winners from the SEC. First, you had Frank Sinkwich at Georgia [1942]. Then there was Billy Cannon at LSU [1959]. Finally, there was Steve Spurrier at Florida [1966]. So Pat was trying to become only the fourth SEC player to ever win the Heisman Trophy. Isn't that unbelievable? Pat was the fourth ever."

As Auburn was about to clinch its victory in Athens, Yearout forced a fumble as time wound down in the fourth quarter. "So I'm chasing down Georgia's quarterback and I slap the ball from his hand," Yearout remembered.

Now, he may've just dropped the thing because he was scared to death I'm coming—me all six feet, 210 pounds. So there it is. The ball's on the ground and I went to scoop it up and run into the end zone. Of course, that was a waste of effort because you couldn't advance a fumble back then.

Auburn players celebrate after knocking off undefeated UGA at Sanford Stadium. *Auburn University Library Special Collections.*

But for some reason, I guess because we were about to beat these boys from Georgia, I try to pick the thing up. Well, I strained my back trying to scoop it and fell to the ground in all sorts of pain. Matter of fact, to this very day, when my back starts hurting over there on its right side, I say to myself, "Dadgummit, that was the ball you tried to get in Athens."

As shadows crept over Sanford Stadium, Yearout stayed on the ground, while Kenny Howard, Auburn's Hall-of-Fame trainer, ran to check on him. Unable to walk off on his own power, Yearout put one arm around Howard and his other around Auburn's assistant trainer. Then, as the three men walked off the field, Tiger fans unleashed a deafening roar from its section in Sanford Stadium.

"I turn to Kenny Howard and say, 'Kenny, the crowd is finally recognizing my play,'" Yearout said. "'They're finally appreciating all the hard work our defense has put in this season.' Kenny says, 'You idiot, they're not recognizing you. Coach Jordan just took Pat out of the game!'"

HENLEY AND SWINFORD

Throughout the Deep South's Oldest Rivalry, most recruiting attention has focused on Auburn signing players from the state of Georgia. It's much rarer for an Alabama kid to commit to UGA. Of the eighty-five scholarship players on Georgia's 2015 roster, only transfer Jake Ganus graduated from high school in Alabama. But on Georgia's 1971 roster, the Bulldogs had a starting cornerback named Gene Swinford who came to Athens to follow the footsteps of his older brother Wayne, who starred in Athens from 1962 to 1964. The Swinfords grew up in Munford, Alabama, a short drive from Terry Henley's home in Oxford. But with Munford too small to field a youth league program, Gene joined a team in the neighboring town.

"Gene and I were always the best of friends," Henley said.

The two were only a month apart in age. They went on recruiting trips together. They wore the same college number (23). They even played professionally on the same team (we'll get to that in a minute). But in 1971, the friends collided on a play that Henley didn't appreciate.

"As a running back, the one thing I couldn't stand was when a defender body-rolled you," Henley said. "You know, took your legs out."

As Henley carried the ball across the right end, Swinford (who had two nicknames: Swine-O and Bama) met the Auburn back near the line of scrimmage. No. 23 went for No. 23's legs. "I was so mad," Henley recalled. "I said, 'Swine-O, why can't you stand up and take me on like a man? Take me on like a man!' Gene said, 'Look, Henley, I tried to help you out. You're so slow I could've dropped you for a two-yard loss.'"

The two stayed close after graduation, both ending up in Atlanta in 1973. Henley moved to the city after signing with the Falcons, but he was cut during training camp. Despite the roster move, Atlanta coaches wanted Henley to continue his career in the Seaboard Football League in Pennsylvania. There was one problem—he didn't want to go alone.

"I called Swine-O and invited him, but Gene said he was dating a girl who drove a Porsche and couldn't go," Henley said. "I told him, 'You know what it is, Gene? You're too chicken. You're afraid these guys in Pennsylvania can outrun you.' Swine-O says, 'By god, you pick me up in the morning.'"

So in 1973, two Alabama boys drove 665 miles to Chambersburg, Pennsylvania, where they lived in a Travelodge Motel for a season. Playing for the Chambersburg Cardinals, Henley made $200 a week, while Swinford earned a modest $75. Unhappy with the difference in pay, Swinford considered leaving the Cardinals to move back to Georgia.

"So I took $50 a week from my check and gave it to Swine-O," Henley said. "I had to keep him up there."

Swinford passed away on March 17, 2005, following a battle with cancer. Henley, now in his mid-sixties, still travels to nearly every Auburn game, home or away, and can't remember the last time he missed a trip to Athens.

Sanford Stadium is enclosed now, so the train tracks can't be used as seats. The stadium also has a third deck, so school buildings no longer tower above the field. But each time Henley enters the ticket gate, images from 1971 are impossible to escape.

"I'll sit down and immediately glance at those rooftops on the west side of Sanford Stadium," Henley said. "You know, it's been forty-five years, but I can't forget that day in Athens. I'll never forget what happened in Athens."

6

NO. 2. TARKENTON TO HERRON

NOVEMBER 14, 1959, GEORGIA 14, AUBURN 13

The 1959 contest was played at Sanford Stadium, marking the start of the home-and-home agreement that stands today. This was the first time Auburn traveled to Athens since 1929.

The evening before the opening round of the 2015 U.S. Open at Chambers Bay, I received an e-mail from Loran Smith: "Call my cell....Now would be good; driving from Portland to Tacoma." So I called. And for fifty-four minutes, I mainly listened.

The University of Georgia icon attended his first Auburn-Georgia game in 1958, the final time it was held in Columbus. But it's the following season that he plainly states as "my favorite Georgia-Auburn game ever played."

In charge of mail delivery at UGA's Payne Hall dormitory, Smith had become close with the 1959 football team. He spent time living with quarterback Francis Tarkenton and referred to guard Pat Dye and many others as personal friends. As a senior, Smith was making a name for himself by interning with Dan Magill in Georgia's Sports Information Department.

On the gridiron, the football team was stunning the Southeastern Conference.

Entering 1959, coach Wallace Butts hadn't won an SEC title in eleven years and recently suffered through records of 3-6-1 (1956), 3-7 (1957) and 4-6 (1958). More than a handful of alumni were calling for Butts to step down, but the luck of the "Little Roundman" began to turn in January 1959, when he was elected president of the American Football Coaches Association, the highest honor a coach could receive. A month later, on

February 13, it was proclaimed "Wally Butts Day" in Athens. Still, on the field, UGA was predicted to continue its losing ways in 1959, picked to finish eighth in a ten-team league by most preseason polls.

"The powerhouse teams in '59 were supposed to be Auburn, LSU and Ole Miss," Smith said. "No one really thought much of Georgia. In fact, Coach Butts admitted before the season that we didn't have any horses."

Horses, of course, referring to star athletes. But after LSU beat Ole Miss, and when both LSU and Auburn were stunned by Tennessee, Georgia hosted Auburn on November 14, 1959, with a chance to earn an improbable conference crown.

The week of the game, more than ten thousand students flooded downtown Athens for the largest pep rally in school history. After all, Auburn was about to enter Sanford Stadium with a 29-1-1 record in its last 31 games. "It was the dogfight of all time," Smith said. "Many believed Auburn was going to come to Athens and pull off the victory."

For much of the game, the Tigers seemed capable. The visiting team led 6–0 at halftime, before Georgia's Charley Britt, who was also UGA's starting quarterback and defensive back, dropped back to receive an Auburn punt. (During the 1959 season, Butts developed two units, known as Britt's Battlers and Tarkenton's Raiders. The Battlers, led by Britt at quarterback, would start each game and were better known for their defense. Tarkenton's unit, which specialized in scoring, would then enter the contest to spark the offense.)

As Britt went to receive the punt, UGA junior Pat Dye made a guarantee to his teammate. "Pat was calling defensive signals and said, 'Charley, you're on your own back there. We're about to block this kick,'" Britt remembered.

But as Auburn lined up to punt, Tigers head coach Ralph "Shug" Jordan called timeout. Auburn went back to its sideline. Georgia's line gathered together. So, Britt, standing alone near midfield, began gazing around Sanford Stadium.

"I've only told this story twice in my life because people don't like to believe stuff like this," Britt said. "I stayed on the field during Auburn's timeout and I'm looking toward the end zone. Well, everyone knows how well-manicured Sanford Stadium is, but I saw one big weed near the goal line."

Sitting in his living room in North Augusta, South Carolina, Britt briefly stopped talking as if he wondered what people would make of his story. Moments later, he finished. "At that point, I got an unbelievably strange feeling that I was going to score right where the weed was," Britt said. "And you know what? As I took the punt across the goal line, I stepped right on that very blade of grass."

Georgia suddenly led 7–6 in front of an overflow crowd of more than fifty-five thousand. Auburn answered, however, after Britt accidentally backed into his own punter, Bobby Walden, with 6:35 remaining in the fourth quarter, causing the "Big Toe from Cairo" to boot the ball off Britt's backside. Auburn recovered on the Bulldogs' one-yard line, and quarterback Bryant Harvard scored to put the visitors ahead, 13–7. As Georgia's offense continued to struggle, Auburn retained possession as the clock ticked to below 3:00. However, while attempting to run out the clock, Harvard made a critical mistake on second down.

"Bryant Harvard faked to the running back going away from me," Pat Dye remembered. "Coming down the line, I had a perfect view of what happened and I saw Harvard pull the ball. I would've caught him behind the line of scrimmage, but he just dropped the ball. Nobody hit him. Nobody touched him. It just came out and I fell on it."

Nearly six decades later, the play remains vivid for Auburn center Jackie Burkett. "All we were trying to do was run the dang clock out," Burkett said. "I mean, Bryant pulled the ball to waste a little more clock and ended up fumbling it. I'll never forget that play. Never."

Georgia had new life at Auburn's thirty-five-yard line. With the clock dwindling and not having scored an offensive touchdown all game, Tarkenton completed a pair of key passes to UGA captain Don Soberdash, which drove Georgia toward Auburn's ten. However, refusing to go quietly, the visiting defense held UGA to minus three yards over the ensuing plays to force UGA into a fourth-down situation from the thirteen. With an SEC championship at stake and twenty seconds to play, Georgia signaled timeout, allowing Tarkenton to design a play in the huddle.

"I'll tell you exactly what was said," Dye recalled. "Bobby Towns was wingback, Bill Herron was tight end on the left. Francis said, 'Bill, you block down for a three count and Bobby, you run a turn-in in front of Auburn's halfback. Bill, after blocking, you run a down-and-out, and as I roll away, I'm gonna hit you for the touchdown.'"

Added Soberdash: "I had already caught two passes on that drive and Francis told me to run to the right on fourth down. Well, when I ran right, it seemed like the entire stadium collapsed on me and Auburn totally forgot about Bill Herron over there on the left."

The play worked to perfection. After Tarkenton rolled right, about a three-count later, he threw across the field to Herron, who calmly snagged

UGA head coach Wallace Butts is carried off the Sanford Stadium field after his team defeated Auburn, 14–13. *University of Georgia Historical Archives Library.*

the game-tying score. Durward Pennington, known as the "Automatic Toe," converted the extra point for a 14–13 victory. UGA was headed to the Orange Bowl.

Following the game, a reporter asked Pennington if he was nervous before kicking the deciding point. "Frankly, no," Pennington said. "I thought we were ahead 13–12."

In a state of elation, one Georgia alumnus, William W. Baxley of Macon, died of a heart attack after the winning score. UGA students stormed the field and were photographed climbing on goalposts.

"I was doing summersaults all over that Cracker Jack press box," said Loran Smith, reminiscing on memories. "But I had to be careful because you could fall out of that thing."

Speaking to reporters after the game, the typically stern Butts said, "There will be no bed-checks tonight. This was the greatest thrill I have received in a lifetime of football." Auburn's Jordan, who was an assistant coach at UGA in the late 1940s, praised his former boss, saying, "If we had to lose. I repeat, if we had to lose, I'm glad it was Wallace Butts who beat us."

In a column for the *Atlanta Journal-Constitution*, Furman Bisher wrote:

The score was 14–13 but that was beside the point. The story was the way it happened, and what happened and the way the whole world seemed to gather in Athens, Ga., for a little while after Durward Pennington kicked the extra point that won. People danced up and down the aisles and out into the streets. Strangers hugged and kissed strangers. Small children raced out on the field to grasp their heroes, wearing the red shirts which their own sweat had turned the rich color of blood. And on the sidelines, a colony of his football players hoisted Wallace Butts on their shoulders and gave their coach the absolutely swellest ride of his long life of coaching ups and downs.

As Sanford Stadium emptied and journalists began leaving the press area, Smith and Magill (UGA sports information director) stayed. After all, there was another game being played in Tuscaloosa. Having kicked off an hour after Auburn and Georgia, Georgia Tech and Alabama were in a battle of their own as nightfall hit Athens.

"Back in those days, Western Union would provide updates to the press box and Dan Magill kept us all informed," Smith said. "Finally, just as it became dark at the stadium, we got word that Alabama had defeated Tech, 9–7."

Smith briefly choked up on the other end of the phone as memories of Magill (who died in 2014 at age ninety-three) came pouring back. Then, somewhere between Portland and Tacoma, he finished the story. "I'll never forget what happened next," Smith said. "Dan Magill hopped on that press box bench, raised both arms and shouted, 'Double header!'"

Following his improbable 10-1 season, Butts was named Coach of the Year in the SEC and became the first coach to receive an invitation to speak at a joint session of the Georgia Assembly. In his address to legislators, Butts said, "Football is the most democratic game in the world. It makes no difference where you come from, or what your race or religion is. There's only one way to become a good football player: That's through hard work and ability. There are no shortcuts. You have to pay the price to be good."

INSIDE THE RIVALRY

Bryant Harvard now raises grass-fed beef in Thomasville, Georgia. He grew up in Thomasville and says he left his home state to play college football for two reasons. "I loved Coach Jordan," Harvard said. "And I loved the culture at Auburn—it reminded me of Thomasville."

Being from Georgia, Harvard admits there was no game he craved winning more than the one against the Bulldogs. However, despite only losing once to UGA, the lone defeat proved costly. "It's a strange thing because there's more conversation about my fumble than about the drive Georgia made to score," Harvard said. "That's always been a puzzle to me. We had a very good defense and Georgia drove nearly forty yards to win that ballgame. I wish more people would appreciate Georgia's touchdown because it didn't come easy."

Looking back on the play, Harvard says he faked a handoff and then bootlegged to the outside. "I was doing a fake, then a bootleg, and I really thought I had a chance to break it all the way if Georgia's end took the fake."

The rest is history: Georgia didn't bite. Bryant fumbled. UGA's offense drove thirty-five yards to clinch its first SEC title since 1948.

"I didn't think it was my fault we lost the ballgame," Harvard said. "It's not like I fumbled on the one-yard line. I fumbled near the forty and Georgia drove and scored a touchdown. Look, I gave Georgia a chance to win but I don't think I lost the ballgame."

Neal Ellis, sportswriter for the *Birmingham News*, printed after the 1959 game, "The Auburn dressing room was sober and quiet as a tomb. The defeated would accept no consolation. They were crushed."

A YEAR LATER IN 1960, GEORGIA TRAVELED to Auburn for the first time in the history of the Deep South's Oldest Rivalry. In anticipation of the game, Auburn paid nearly $500,000 to enclose the south end zone of Cliff Hare Stadium, increasing capacity from 34,500 to 44,500. It was Harvard's senior year, and the Georgia native made up for his miscue in Athens. In front of the largest crowd that had ever witnessed a game in the state of Alabama, Harvard completed a sixteen-yard pass to halfback Jimmy Burson late in the fourth quarter, and kicker Ed Dyas made a field goal with forty-two seconds remaining to propel the Tigers to a 9–6 victory.

"Coach Jordan told the press, 'You guys blamed Bryant for losing the game last year—you need to give him credit for winning this one,'" Harvard recalled. "I really appreciated that compliment, but Coach Jordan never did blame me for what happened in '59. You know, after the fumble I was still able to go to class and Auburn still fed me."

When asked about the legendary finishes in 1959 and 1960, Jordan sarcastically said in 1960, "Maybe we should start charging $10 a fan to see Auburn and Georgia play." Tickets in 1960 were five dollars.

For Jackie Burkett, it's not losing to Georgia in 1959 that still haunts him. It's how Auburn was treated prior to the SEC-deciding contest.

"I've played a lot of football in my lifetime and the worst thing that I've ever experienced was waiting to go on Georgia's field in 1959," he recalled.

> We were about to run out, and their fans started hitting us with chicken bones and garbage. I'm talking about fresh chicken bones were bouncing off our heads and helmets. When I have nightmares about football, that 1959 game is the one that comes up—unbelievable. That was the grossest thing I've ever seen in my life and I'll tell you one thing: that would never happen in Auburn.

When asked if Burkett has returned to Athens since 1959, the former lineman and member of Auburn's Walk of Fame said, "No. I never will."

7

NO. 3. THE PRAYER AT JORDAN-HARE

NOVEMBER 16, 2013, AUBURN 43, GEORGIA 38

T here aren't many times in sports when you wake up on Sunday morning and know you'll never forget the night before. There are fewer times when you leave a stadium and think, *This rivalry has been played 117 times. And I just witnessed the most stunning ending there's ever been.*

Forget for a moment about Auburn's final touchdown: the seventy-three-yard miracle pass from Nick Marshall to Ricardo Louis. As historic as the

Nick Marshall (14) attempts a pass against UGA in 2013. *Morris Communications.*

play was, what made it even more improbable was how far the Tigers had come in twelve months. A season before, Auburn went 0-8 in the SEC, fired coach Gene Chizik and lost by a combined 87–0 to Georgia and Alabama. With largely the same group of players on its roster, most everyone outside of Auburn's locker room assumed 2013 would be another struggle on the Plains. Instead, it ended with a Southeastern Conference championship.

THE QUARTERBACK

In August 2015, Nick Marshall had just finished his fourth day of NFL training camp when the Jacksonville Jaguars director of media relations pointed him my way. Journalists swarmed Blake Bortles, Julius Thomas and Marcedes Lewis, but no one else wanted the undrafted rookie. It was just us two, standing in Jacksonville's summer heat.

For about twenty minutes, we spoke about the 2013 Auburn-Georgia game—the pass, the tip, the catch. But before Jordan-Hare Stadium erupted, Marshall remembered the eerie silence as he faced fourth-and-eighteen, seventy-three yards from Georgia's end zone. "I'll never forget our huddle," Marshall said. "Ricardo looked me dead in the eye and said, 'Throw me the ball. I'll make a play, throw me the ball.' Right then, I decided where I was going."

As the play unfolded, Louis drew a double team, as receiver Sammie Coates went uncovered over the middle of the field. By all accounts, Coates—who was supposed to be Marshall's primary read—was the right choice. He was the logical target. But like Marshall's path to Auburn, he didn't take the conventional route.

As a two-sport standout from Pineview, Georgia, Marshall led Wilcox County High to the 2009 Class A state championship, its lone football title in school history. But it was the fall of 2006, when Marshall was playing junior varsity as an eighth grader, that Wilcox County coaches first got a glimpse of the future. In an October game at Turner County, the fourteen-year-old injured his ribs early in the contest and was forced to sit out most of the game. However, trailing 24–21 with less than ninety seconds to play, Marshall approached JV coach Clint Bloodsworth.

"Nick took a good lick in the second quarter, but came to me before our final drive and said, 'Coach, I can go back,'" said Bloodsworth, who was also

Marshall's middle school basketball coach. Turner County was composed largely of tenth graders and seemed destined to beat the younger and smaller Wilcox County squad. But as the clock ticked below thirty seconds, Marshall rolled left, planted his back foot and soared a forty yard pass toward six-foot, six-inch ninth grader Lonnie Outlaw.

"Lonnie caught it on the one-yard line, then fell in for the game-winning score," Bloodsworth said. "It was the most exciting JV game I ever saw. Heck, it was probably the most exciting JV game ever played."

Fast-forward to 2009, and Wilcox County was again leaving its coaches mesmerized. Although the Patriots failed to win its own region title after losing 48–14 to Twiggs County—a game Marshall missed after suffering back spasms before kickoff—once the state playoffs began, the quarterback again foreshadowed his ability to create miracles.

In the first round, Wilcox County trailed late in the fourth quarter before rallying to beat Treutlen High, 23–20. In the second round, Marshall's team upset Greenville High (previously 11-0), 39–13. It was the only playoff game in which Wilcox County didn't trail in the fourth quarter.

Following its rout over Greenville, Wilcox County traveled to Atlanta to face reigning Class A champion Wesleyan. "You talk about fish being outta water," said Mark Ledford, head coach of Wilcox County. "We're from the country. *The country.* So we leave here and go to Wesleyan, who had the nicest stadium we ever played in. A campus like that was something we'd never seen." Ledford's team struggled offensively against the defending state champions before his junior quarterback found Nate Moorhouse for a 30-yard score. Marshall completed twenty-four of forty-one passes for 275 yards, handing Wesleyan its first defeat in twenty-four games.

In the semifinals, on a cold, rainy night in Homerville, Georgia, Wilcox County trailed 14–12 with 3:17 remaining. However, one play after a Clinch County punt, Marshall connected on an eighty-yard touchdown with Outlaw, the same combination that had provided JV heroics in 2006. The 20–14 victory earned Wilcox County a trip to the Georgia Dome, a place Marshall had dreamed about playing since grammar school. Across the street from his Pineview home, Marshall, his younger brother Quez Mahoganey and childhood friend Tay Porter would spend countless hours in a vacant field throwing any ball they could find. "It was just an empty pasture," Ledford said. "An empty lot. But as kids, Nick, Tay and Quez called that field the Georgia Dome."

On December 12, 2009, Marshall arrived at the real Georgia Dome to face undefeated Savannah Christian. With a title at stake, Wilcox County trailed 21–14 midway through the fourth quarter before Marshall and Porter transformed their childhood dreams into reality. Like so many afternoons at home, Marshall heaved a fifty-two-yard pass toward Porter. The receiver momentarily lost the ball while falling down, then corralled it as he lay on his back at the four-yard line. On the next play, Marshall scored on a quarterback scramble. Wilcox County won, 30–21, while Savannah Christian head coach Donald Chumley called Marshall the best quarterback he'd ever seen.

"Every game is winnable when you have Nick Marshall," Ledford said. "He's a winner. An absolute winner. No play was ever too big for Nick."

MARSHALL WAS TWICE NAMED MIDDLE GEORGIA Offensive Player of the Year by the *Macon Telegraph* and was part of UGA's so-called "Dream Team" recruiting class of 2011. Switching from quarterback to defensive back, Marshall spent one season in Athens, earning the nickname "Dr. Death" because of his impressive cornerback skills in practice. (The name was taken from a 1986 movie, *The Best of Times*, starring Robin Williams.) But Marshall was dismissed before Dr. Death could translate his skills from the Woodruff practice fields to Sanford Stadium. On February 3, 2012, Marshall and two freshman teammates (safety Chris Sanders and receiver Sanford Seay) were removed from the team after an alleged dorm-room theft. In a statement, Georgia coach Mark Richt wrote:

> *It's a privilege to play college football and to be a part of this team and University. Along with that privilege comes certain responsibilities. Mistakes were made, and part of our job is helping them learn from mistakes. Going forward, we are committed to assisting them find opportunities where they can continue their education.*

Less than twenty-four hours after being dismissed, Marshall arrived at Wilcox County High to meet with Ledford. For about an hour, the two rode in Ledford's pickup while mapping what the next step should be. "Eventually, Nick goes, 'Coach, I wanna go back and play the position that got me here. I wanna play JUCO for a season and then be a quarterback in the SEC,'" Ledford recalled. "I looked at him and said, 'OK.'"

The same day, Ledford received a call from Jeff Tatum, head coach of Garden City Community College. Tatum was previously the offensive coordinator at Georgia Military College and had established a strong relationship with Ledford.

Marshall had been dismissed from UGA on a Friday, and by Monday morning, Ledford was driving his former star to meet Tatum. "I picked Nick up at his house and we went to meet Coach Tatum," Ledford said. "Coach Tatum had left Garden City on Sunday and we met him off the interstate in Jasper, Alabama."

Marshall never unpacked his bags after leaving UGA. Upon reaching Jasper, the two coaches pulled into a gas station off Interstate 22, where Marshall removed his luggage from Ledford's truck and put it in Tatum's.

"Before switching from my vehicle to Coach Tatum's, Nick peeled off the Georgia sticker from his little refrigerator," Ledford said.

By the time Marshall and Tatum reached Tupelo, Mississippi, Marshall had already registered for classes at Garden City. That Tuesday, he was officially enrolled. Having switched to quarterback, Marshall reappeared on the radar of Auburn receivers coach Dameyune Craig, who had recruited him while Craig was at Florida State. In the end, Marshall committed to Auburn without ever seeing campus.

MARSHALL'S WINDING ROAD HAD STRAIGHTENED in the fall of 2013. Now thriving in Gus Malzahn's offense, the signal-caller propelled Auburn to a 9-1 record entering November 16, 2013—Marshall's first game against his former team. "I played every game at Auburn with a chip on my shoulder," Marshall said. "But the biggest chip I ever played with was 2013 against Georgia."

For three quarters, UGA's defense failed to stop Marshall, as Auburn led 37–17 with less than ten minutes remaining. Then, Aaron Murray awoke. His five-yard strike to Rantavious Wooten made it 37–24 with 9:35 to play. A twenty-four-yard completion to Arthur Lynch made it a one-possession game with 5:59 left. Finally, Murray's five-yard scamper gave Georgia a 38–37 advantage with 1:49 remaining.

"We never panicked," Marshall said. "We never thought we were going to lose."

The same couldn't be said for Ledford. As Marshall's high school coach watched from the section next to Georgia's Redcoat Marching Band, he could feel Auburn's momentum slip away.

"It became very hard to watch," Ledford admitted. "The Redcoats kept playing, people were saying things, and all I thought about was how hard Nick was gonna take this loss. I felt sick."

As the time dwindled, Georgia's defense stood tall, forcing Marshall into a fourth-and-eighteen from his twenty-seven-yard line. With thirty-six seconds left, UGA called timeout to assemble a final formation.

"The look I saw in Ricardo's eyes before we left the huddle," said Marshall, before pausing. "I had never seen that in a teammate before. I could tell how bad he wanted to make a play."

As for Ledford, he assumed defeat was imminent, which would have ended Auburn's dream of an SEC title. "I had become pretty upset in the stands," he admitted. "I told my wife, 'Get your stuff because after this play we're getting out of here.' She just looked at me and said, 'You're such a pessimist—just wait and see.' I said, 'No, come on.' So we had everything in our hands and we were ready to leave."

Electing to target Louis, Marshall bypassed an open Coates and heaved the football into a sea of red and black. However, as safety Tray Matthews position himself to make the game-ending interception, teammate Josh Harvey-Clemons tipped it away, floating the ball into the still air of Jordan-Hare Stadium. Louis hauled in the deflection for a seventy-three-yard score.

"The next day watching film, Coach Malzahn asked, 'Did you not see Sammie?'" Marshall recalled. "I told him I put my trust in Ricardo. He just smiled and said, 'Hey, it worked out.'"

Ledford promptly returned to his seat and watched as Marshall etched his name into Auburn-Georgia lore.

"I thought to myself, 'Oh my god,'" Ledford said. "'He did it again.'"

While sprinting to celebrate with Louis, Marshall lifted two fingers, symbolizing that Auburn needed to attempt a two-point conversion. The conversion failed, but Marshall's awareness didn't go unnoticed by Ledford. "You and me, we would've been jumping in the stands to find our family," Ledford said. "What was Nick doing? He was thinking about the next play."

That sweltering morning in Jacksonville, Marshall enjoyed reminiscing on "The Prayer at Jordan-Hare." But looking back—whether in football or life—isn't something he does often. In the years since the play, outside of mandatory film sessions, Marshall admits he's never watched a replay. He has no pictures or keepsakes from the miraculous ending and says, "Once it's over, it's over." But don't confuse Marshall's ability to look ahead as lacking appreciation for what he accomplished. Standing on the Jaguars practice field, it was clear that no longer being in college was difficult for Marshall. Time after time, he brought up Auburn teammates. Time after time, he talked about texting players, including Louis, just to see how things were going.

"I miss Auburn a lot," Marshall said. "People in Auburn say I'm great or even a legend, but I don't look at it like that. I was just a quarterback—just Auburn's quarterback."

The Receiver

Ricardo Louis never broke stride. Not as the ball was about to be hauled in by Tray Matthews. Not as it was tipped in the air by Josh Harvey-Clemons.

"At first, I thought about jumping for it," Louis said.

Instead, he did what Auburn receivers coach Dameyune Craig preached to his personnel. "Coach Craig always tells us to look the ball in," Louis said. "Just look the ball in. Coach Craig was the reason why I caught that ball."

The play—originally coined "Little Rock"—was designed by Malzahn in 1998, while he was head coach at Shiloh Christian High in Arkansas. Little Rock was where the high school state championship game was played, and Malzahn used the play in the 1998 title contest against Hector High. In 1998, Shiloh Christian completed the dig route (Coates's route in 2013) and went on to capture Malzahn's first state title. This time, however, the open dig route was bypassed in favor of Louis, who was running a post.

"I had never played outside receiver in that set before," Louis said. "Coach Malzahn just told me, 'Go make a play.'"

Earlier that week, Malzahn told reporters he had an inkling that Louis would make a big play in a big game. Still, the enormity of Louis's touchdown was tough for the receiver to comprehend.

"It's like a dream," Louis said. "When the ball got tipped, I was looking in the air and then I finally spotted it. All game, I kept saying, 'Get the ball in my hands. I'll make a play!' But I never expected it to be like that."

After the touchdown, Georgia still had twenty-five seconds with which to answer. And the Bulldogs nearly did. Behind Murray's arm, UGA marched to Auburn's twenty-five-yard line and had eight seconds to score. With two shots at the end zone, Murray's first attempt sailed right of Jonathon Rumph at the goal line.

On the final play, Auburn defensive end Dee Ford plowed into Murray's side, and the ball fell harmlessly on the eight-yard line.

Auburn running back Tre Mason celebrates after beating Georgia in 2013. *Morris Communications.*

HOW THEY REMEMBERED "THE PRAYER AT JORDAN-HARE"

UGA coach Mark Richt:

> *I literally hit my knees and then my chest hit on the ground. I was like, "What in the world is going on?" That would have been the greatest comeback in the history of Georgia football. It actually was. We were down 20 in the fourth and came back and took the lead. So we did erase the deficit.*

Wilcox County coach Mark Ledford:

> *After the game, we waited for the players to come out and I walked with Nick [Marshall] back to his dorm. We were walking and I said, "Nick, you understand what you just did, right?" He just looked at me and said, "What's that, Coach?"*

Rod Bramblett, voice of the Auburn Tigers:

> *It's one of my least favorite calls because it completely caught me off guard. Being a play-by-play guy, something like that should never catch you off guard. I will say this though—the call definitely captured the emotion. I think it captured the emotion even more so than the Alabama play* [Chris Davis's 109-yard field goal returned for a touchdown] *two weeks later.*

UGA quarterback Aaron Murray:

> *It's like a nightmare and you just want to wake up.*

Rhett Lashlee, Auburn's offensive coordinator:

> *How did I grade the play with Nick? Good job. Just like we drew it up. Yeah, he didn't get a minus for that.*

Former Auburn head coach Pat Dye:

> *Auburn shouldn't have been in a position to make a play like that. I still don't think [Aaron] Murray scored on that fourth-down run. I was*

looking at it on replay and the official on the goal line, he stepped on the up-field side of the goal line. He walked out there, then walked back over and signaled touchdown. Look, it was close and I agree there wasn't enough evidence to overturn it, but I don't think Murray scored. As for the catch, it was just a fluke thing. But I will say one thing about Ricardo Louis: He didn't quit playing. He kept running.

Auburn coach Gus Malzahn, moments after the win:

This is definitely a Waffle House night.

8

NO. 4. 70-X TAKEOFF

NOVEMBER 16, 2002, GEORGIA 24, AUBURN 21

When people ask, "What was the biggest win you were ever part of?" 2002 at Auburn was the one.
—*David Greene*

Mark Richt lifted his hand and signaled a bid of $1,000 to the auctioneer. He did it again, and again, and again. Finally, as guests attending Georgia's 2015 Fellowship of Christian Athletes Gala realized their coach wasn't going to lose, Richt pointed to the stage a final time. "Ten-thousand dollars," he said. "There's no telling where I'd be right now if that play never happened."

The item at stake was an eighty-four- by thirty-six-inch painting by artist Steve Penley depicting UGA receiver Michael Johnson leaping for the game-winning touchdown at Jordan-Hare Stadium. Or, as Athens calls it, "70-X Takeoff."

Although Johnson's reception is the game's most famous play, it's not always the first memory that comes to Richt's mind. Entering 2002, Georgia had never played in an SEC championship game—a contest established in 1992. In addition, it had been twenty years since UGA won a conference title. But, as November 16, 2002, approached, Georgia was one win away from clinching the SEC East and securing a trip to Atlanta.

"That whole season we talked about breaking through the glass ceiling," offensive lineman Jon Stinchcomb said. "Our 1998 [recruiting] class was special and we wanted to be the catalyst for change. We wanted to be the

Michael Johnson hauls in the game-winning reception over Horace Willis in 2002. The ball remains encased inside UGA's Butts-Mehre Building. *Morris Communications.*

ones to help our university win its first conference title since 1982."

Needing a win at Auburn to represent the Eastern Division, Georgia struggled the opening thirty minutes, trailing 14–3 at halftime. As UGA made its way to the locker room, the coaches met alone to discuss adjustments, while players took a moment to deliberate among themselves. Sensing their championship dreams slipping away, Stinchcomb didn't wait for second-year coach Mark Richt to enter the room.

"It's hard to remember my exact words," Stinchcomb said. "But I'll put it like this. The first half wasn't heading the direction we wanted. There was a lot at stake and I kept thinking about that glass ceiling of not being able to play for an SEC title. I thought back to all the blood, sweat and tears our team had sacrificed. It all came out."

To this day, Stinchcomb's speech is remembered by his 2002 teammates and coaches, although none would repeat exactly what was said. I could tell Stinchcomb remembered more than he would let on, but as I pressed for details, he smiled and humbly praised teammates. "I wasn't the only one that said something at halftime," he said. "Boss [Bailey] got the defense fired up, too."

To be fair, others did speak, but years later, it's Stinchcomb's words that still resonate. While at events together, Richt often introduces Stinchcomb by referencing the halftime delivery. Even after purchasing Penley's painting at the FCA banquet, Richt stood in front of the gallery and immediately brought up his lineman's message.

Jason Campbell (17) stiff-arms a helmet-less Ken Veal in 2002. Veal's pressure forced an incomplete pass on the play. *Morris Communications.*

"I was meeting with the coaches but I could hear what Jon was saying," Richt said. "When I got to the locker room, I didn't need to say anything. Jon had already said it all."

Stinchcomb's teammates haven't forgotten, either. Quarterback David Greene said: "Jon's speech certainly had a sense of urgency. He was able to give us that fire and momentum we needed to really make things happen in the second half."

Wide receiver Damien Gary recalled: "As a younger guy on the team, when a guy like Jon spoke, we listened. His speech came from the heart, and after he finished, we knew we could do it. Jon led us to victory and we followed."

Offensive lineman Dennis Roland said, "I can still see Jon standing on a locker, pouring his heart out to the team. That was a special, special moment."

Offensive lineman Kevin Breedlove: "The bottom line is we were playing flat and Stinch knew that. Being our captain and leader of the offensive line, he stepped up and displayed his leadership qualities when we needed them most. I remember him saying, 'We're not going out like this. We're going out there and winning the SEC East.'"

DESPITE RALLYING FOR FOURTEEN THIRD-QUARTER POINTS, Georgia still trailed 21–17 with 1:58 remaining. With twenty years of title-less seasons weighing on the Classic City, Greene had one drive to revive a once dominant program—to provide Georgia with that elusive trip to the Georgia Dome.

Quite simply, the Bulldogs answer came from an unlikely hero. Entering the game, junior Michael Johnson had totaled eleven receptions through the first ten games of 2002, but injuries to Damien Gary and Terrence Edwards forced Johnson into a starring role. "All night, Michael had the hot hand," Greene said. "He had [twelve] receptions before the catch everyone remembers."

Safety Sean Jones began the final drive with a punt return to Georgia's forty-one-yard line. Fred Gibson brought UGA to within striking distance with a forty-one-yard reception to Auburn's fourteen. Greene, however, fired incomplete on first down. A false start made it second and fifteen. Consecutive incompletions on second and third downs left the Bulldogs in need of a miracle.

With the season one play from slipping away, Georgia faced fourth and fifteen from Auburn's nineteen-yard line and needed a touchdown to reach Atlanta. To Greene's surprise, Richt called 70-X Takeoff, a play Georgia hadn't run all year. "Normally we called 70 Takeoff, which gave me an option to look to either receiver," Greene said. "But when Coach Richt added the X, that was his way of saying, 'Throw it to Michael Johnson.'"

Looking back on the play, Greene remembers freezing Junior Rosegreen, Auburn's hard-hitting safety, before lobbing the ball toward the back-left pylon. "When I pumped, the safety flat-footed and never moved to Michael's side," Greene said. "Then Michael made one of the greatest catches in Georgia history."

Johnson's catch over Horace Willis put the Bulldogs in front 24–21 with eighty-five seconds left. Auburn was unable to answer. After hauling in the touchdown, Johnson was mobbed by teammates, while Willis—who had committed to UGA before switching to Auburn—knelt on both knees.

"As a lineman, I was trying to listen to the crowd to know what the result of the play was," Breedlove said. "All of the sudden, I heard the air completely go out of the stadium. At that point, I knew something really good had happened."

Johnson, a native of Tulsa, Oklahoma, finished with a career-high thirteen receptions for 141 yards and was named SEC Player of the Week. For Greene, the significance of the play didn't hit him on the field or in the locker room. For a kid whose grandfather, father and sister all went to Auburn, it took a little longer to appreciate the history that had been written at Jordan-Hare Stadium.

"I remember sitting on the bus and replaying the game in my head," Greene said. "That's when I thought, 'Did that really just happen? Did we really just win that game?'"

Three weeks later, Georgia beat Arkansas in the Georgia Dome to capture the school's first conference title since 1982. UGA, who finished ranked No. 3 in the BCS rankings, defeated Florida State in the Sugar Bowl.

Ken Veal Looks Back

As fondly as UGA defensive tackle Ken Veal recalls clinching the SEC East title, his postgame memories were less about football and more on his mother's experience at Jordan-Hare Stadium.

Renee Veal, who donned a No. 96 jersey during the game, became the focal point of a particular Auburn fan each time her son tallied one of his eight tackles. "Throughout the game, this Auburn supporter kept making rude comments to my mom," said Veal, known by teammates as "Pooh." "Well, after the play when my helmet came off and I caused Jason Campbell to throw an incomplete pass, the guy made one more ugly comment."

At that point, a Georgia fan sitting near Veal's mother took the matter into his own hands, and a physical altercation broke out near Renee. In the end, both the Auburn and UGA instigators were ejected for fighting.

"The Georgia fan was with two buddies, and one turned to my mom and said, 'Don't worry, we'll bail him out after the game,'" Veal said. "They turned right back and continued watching as if nothing happened. My mom was dumbfounded but very grateful."

9

NO. 5. AUBURN STUNS NO. 1 GEORGIA

NOVEMBER 21, 1942, AUBURN 27, GEORGIA 13

Over on the Plains there is silence. Coach Jack Meagher's refusal to say much at all about the coming game is a sign of one of two things: He either is brewing something unpleasant for the Bulldogs or he has given up all hope. And all that think the latter could probably be filled comfortably in the nearest telephone booth.
—*Joe Livingston, sports editor of the* Columbus Ledger, *1942*

In the fall of 1942, the nation's focus was on World War II, as many college football players were only months away from enlisting in the service. Japan's attack on Pearl Harbor occurred a year before, and the United States had already sent troops into the Pacific. However, with the world largely preparing for battle, Athens was experiencing its greatest football season since being introduced to the game in 1892. Southern sports writers had labeled Georgia's 1942 squad as Wallace Butts's dream team—an offensive machine unlike anything the school had produced, highlighted by Heisman Trophy winner Frank Sinkwich, halfback Charley Trippi and winners of fifteen straight games heading into November 21, 1942. Earlier in the season, UGA beat Florida, 75–0, to climb its way to No. 1 in the nation.

On the Plains, the Tigers were unfolding an entirely different script. Auburn entered the contest 4-4-1, prompting an Associated Press article to suggest, "Some fans might argue on paper that Auburn should lose by 81 points, since Georgia won 75–0 over Florida, which had beaten Auburn 6–0." Auburn, double-digit underdogs, was also at a disadvantage in the personnel department. Only nineteen players made the trip from the Plains

Above: Monk Gafford (25) runs past Georgia's defense in 1942. *Auburn University Library Special Collections.*

Left: Auburn head coach Jack Meagher installed a unique offense to defeat heavily favored Georgia. *Auburn University Library Special Collections.*

to Columbus because of military obligations. Thirty-eight Georgia players arrived by train.

One of the Tigers serving his country was assistant coach Ralph "Shug" Jordan, who was stationed in North Africa. However, nearly two years before departing for service, Jordan had discovered a tip in Sinkwich's alignment that predetermined whether Georgia had called a running or passing play. In 1941, Auburn held UGA to seven points, but still lost, 7–0. In 1942, the Tigers again relied on Jordan's discovery. As Auburn's defense kept a keen eye on Sinkwich, Georgia was limited to thirty-seven rushing yards, while the Heisman Trophy winner completed just twelve of thirty-four passes.

After the Tigers upset UGA in 1942, Auburn business manager of athletics Jeff Beard produced an extra copy of the game film and sent it to Africa for Jordan to watch during World War II. According to an *Atlanta Journal* article by Sam Heys, a proud Jordan replayed it throughout the war, prompting Butts to say, "I wish you all would win another game so you could get new film."

On top of Jordan's scouting, Auburn head coach Jack Meagher installed a unique offense to face Georgia. For years, Auburn ran the single wing, but for the 1942 contest it unveiled a "T" formation with a varied package of misdirections. Meagher—an Irish Catholic known as "Whispering Jack" because he rarely raised his voice at players—also used newspaper writers as a way of further confusing the heavily favored Bulldogs. Two days before kickoff in Columbus, Meagher told reporters he planned to rely heavily on the pass and had players run aerial drills in front of local journalists.

Turns out, it was all mind games. Auburn never completed a pass, but compiled 355 rushing yards to grind its way through the No. 1 Bulldogs. Tailback Roy "Monk" Gafford led the charge with 119 yards and a score, and fans rushed the field as time expired. Tiger supporters tore down both goalposts and proceeded to carry Gafford off the Memorial Stadium turf. In excitement over Auburn's victory, Alabama newspapers boasted how the final score wasn't indicative of just how badly the Bulldogs were outplayed. Bob Phillips of the *Birmingham News* wrote: "The Tigers from the Loveliest Village of the Plains, a two-touchdown underdog with not too many takers, crushed the great Georgia eleven 27 to 13 in the greatest upset of an upset-studded football season. And it wasn't even close."

The *Montgomery Advertiser* mocked UGA, saying Georgia's bowl hopes could be seen "gradually floating across the Chattahoochee in the late afternoon breeze."

As high praise flowed endlessly through Alabama newspapers, the Georgia media was equally as distraught. The *Columbus Ledger-Enquirer* went as far as saying, "There is no doubt that the thing Mighty Monk Gafford lured his mates into doing is the worst fate that has befell the state of Georgia since Sherman." A headline printed in the *Atlanta Constitution* read, "Auburn blasts Georgia's Rose Bowl dreams, 27–13." Then there was the front page of the *Athens Banner-Herald*, whose first two sentences said it all: "You may bow in silent meditation today for a football empire that was. Georgia lost Saturday to a brilliant and underrated Auburn, 27–13, and the crash of America's No. 1 football team probably resounded all the way to Pasadena, Calif."

A week later, Georgia bounced back from the defeat with a 34–0 rout over Georgia Tech to become SEC champions and earn that coveted bid to Pasadena. At the Rose Bowl, the Bulldogs—who elected to claim the 1942 national championship—prevailed over UCLA, while finishing No. 2 in the Associated Press rankings behind ranked Ohio State.

In the book *No Ifs, No Ands, A Lot of Butts: 21 Years of Georgia Football*, authors Ed Thilenius and Jim Koger detailed the final 1942 rankings that left Butts and UGA stranded at No. 2. On page 98, they wrote:

> *Bobby Dodd, assistant to [Georgia] Tech coach Bill Alexander, called Georgia the "greatest team in the country." And there were others who agreed with Bobby. Many voters in many polls were cast in favor of the Bulldogs the following week, but in the big one that counted, the Associated Press balloting, the Bulldogs had to be content with second place, being nosed-out on election day by Ohio State.*

For Coach Jack Meagher, tailback Monk Gafford and the rest of Auburn's team, they have no hardware to show from 1942. After the season, Meagher, who fought as a Marine in World War I, was fired by Auburn before again serving his country. In nine years patrolling Auburn's sideline, Meagher never finished higher than third in the SEC. However, as tears streamed down his face on November 21, 1942, the coach had stunned college football.

Meagher's upset stands as the rivalry's greatest.

10

NO. 6. RANDY CAMPBELL BRINGS SUGAR TO ATHENS

NOVEMBER 12, 1983, AUBURN 13, GEORGIA 7

The stakes surrounding Auburn's 1983 trip to Athens were no secret: A chance at the school's first SEC title since 1957, a trip to the Sugar Bowl and dethroning Georgia as conference champions. Randy Campbell, however, did have a secret. Hidden in Campbell's suitcase, the senior quarterback brought a packet of Domino sugar from Auburn's Sewell Hall cafeteria.

"I didn't tell anyone," Campbell said. "And if we lost, no one would've ever known."

The packet made its way from the Plains to Athens, then from Auburn's team hotel (the Holiday Inn) in Madison, Georgia, to Sanford Stadium. Decades later, its final destination is one of Campbell's fondest memories.

BEFORE SUGAR POURED

Georgia was in the midst of its greatest stretch in school history. Vince Dooley's dynasty hadn't lost an SEC game since November 17, 1979, and a victory over his alma mater would make it four straight conference titles. Then there was Auburn. In Pat Dye's third season, the Tigers were a victory shy of completing the program's historic turnaround and clinching an SEC crown for the first time in twenty-six years.

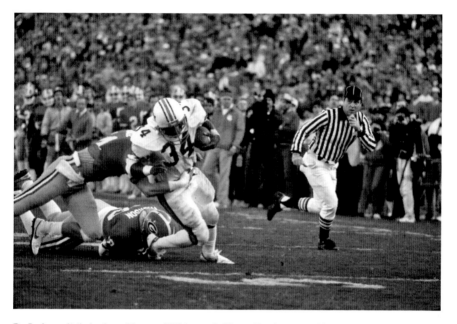

Bo Jackson (34) sheds tacklers as UGA coach Vince Dooley urges his team to bring down the sophomore running back. *Auburn University Library Special Collections.*

"Auburn was the up-and-coming program after Pat Dye took over," said UGA quarterback John Lastinger. "They were pretty good Dye's first year in '81. They improved in '82. And by '83 Auburn was really, really good."

The Monday before playing Auburn, Dooley asked UGA assistant coach Alex Gibbs to present a scouting report on the Tigers. Gibbs, Georgia's offensive line coach, had been Auburn's offensive coordinator from 1979 to 1981 and figured to have inside information on his former players.

"When giving the report, Coach Gibbs didn't write a name for Auburn's nose guard [Dowe Aughtman] or two tackles [Doug Smith and Donnie Humphrey]," Lastinger said. "He simply wrote: Godzilla 1, Godzilla 2 and Godzilla 3. I just put my head down and thought, 'Oh, wow.'"

THE GAME

By nearly all accounts, the final score deserved to be more convincing. No. 3 Auburn out-rushed Georgia 261 to 51, nearly doubled the time of possession (38:59 to 21:01) and shut out the No. 4 Bulldogs for three quarters. Sparked by a four-yard score from Lionel "Little Train" James—one of thirty-one Georgians playing for the Tigers—Auburn jumped ahead 7–0 with 4:34 remaining in the first period. Continuing to ride the legs of James and sophomore Bo Jackson, the visitors added a pair of Al Del Greco field goals to make it 13–0 at intermission. But as much as the game was dominated by Auburn, Del Greco's right leg ultimately proved costly. Entering the contest, Del Greco had missed just once in nine games and was perfect from within forty yards. But his consistency vanished in Athens. The senior came up short on a fifty-two-yard attempt in the first half. Then, with Auburn looking to secure an SEC title, Del Greco missed twice in the fourth quarter (both from thirty yards), which rejuvenated hope inside Sanford Stadium.

Still trailing 13–0, Georgia abandoned its ground attack and let Lastinger do damage through the air. Georgia threw. And threw. And threw. Eight consecutive times, Dooley elected to pass, and in eighty-four seconds, Georgia had marched eighty yards to Auburn's end zone. "Almost out of desperation, we went to a four-receiver offense and went straight down the field," Lastinger said. "Auburn obviously hadn't prepared for it, because they were all screaming at each other."

To no one's surprise, with 2:11 remaining, both teams lined up for an onside kick, which UGA's David Painter recovered. After controlling the game for fifty-seven minutes, the outcome was now out of Campbell's control.

"I thought I was going to die on the sideline," Campbell said. "I felt so responsible for not putting the game away—for not being able to score touchdowns."

Del Greco was also suffering. Unable to escape the thought of three misfires, Auburn's kicker began to tear up on the sideline as defeat was forty-six yards away. However, as Sanford Stadium roared, so did Auburn's defense. Led by a first-down sack from Quency Williams, the Dogs lost six yards over their final four plays, and the game was decided. Gone were Georgia's hopes of an undefeated season. Born was Dye's first Southeastern Conference title. With a celebration underway, Campbell and Bo Jackson each took a piece of Georgia's hedges, while Jackson stuck it in his mouth and claimed it tasted like dog meat. Inside Auburn's dressing room, Jackson wore a shirt that read "Go Bo."

"That was such a huge win for our program," Campbell said. "To be able to win that game for Coach Dye was unbelievable. It was almost like we were doing it for him."

As the clock hit 0:00, Dye was carried off Georgia's field, the same grass where he had been named an All-American twenty-four years before.

Lionel James (6) scores the go-ahead touchdown for Auburn at Sanford Stadium. James, a native of Albany, Georgia, had a street named "Little Train Lane" after him in his hometown. *Auburn University Library Special Collections.*

WAITING IN THE LOCKER ROOM FOR DYE was a surprise from his quarterback. In one hand, Campbell was carrying a game ball. In the other, he clinched his secret.

"I opened that pack of sugar and sprinkled it on the ball," Campbell said. "Coach Dye licked it right off!"

Auburn finished the season with a Sugar Bowl victory over Michigan and a No. 1 ranking in the *New York Times* poll. The school, however, has elected not to claim the national title. Miami was named No. 1 in the Associated Press poll after upsetting Nebraska in the Orange Bowl.

"We played the toughest schedule in the nation," Dye said. "That's the reason the *New York Times* computer poll voted us the No. 1. That poll didn't have any human element."

Looking back on 1983, Dye says his team improved as the year went on, closing on a ten-game winning streak after losing on September 17 to Texas. Auburn, Miami and Nebraska all finished 11-1. Georgia finished 10-1-1. "The reason the thing turned out how it did was 100-percent television," Dye said. "ABC promoted Miami-Nebraska as the national championship game for a month during the Christmas holiday. If ABC didn't do that, I really believe we would have been No. 1."

As for Randy Campbell, little did he know that 1983 was just the beginning of his personal Auburn-Georgia rivalry. In 1986, he met his wife, Nancy, a University of Georgia alumnus. "My wife's a big-time Dog," Campbell said. "I mean, diehard Dog. The first game we ever went to was 1986 when we hosed them down. I didn't think I'd get another date after that."

In 1992, Campbell became an assistant coach under Dye, putting Nancy in an awkward position during the week of the Deep South's Oldest Rivalry.

"On Wednesday nights, our wives ate dinner with us at Sewell Hall because we'd be watching film and working late," Campbell recalled. "So Nancy was in the lobby waiting for me and Coach Dye comes in. He walks up to her and says, 'Who you pulling for this week?' And Nancy, she's so quick, she looks right back at Coach Dye and goes, 'I don't know Coach, who are you gonna pull for?' Coach Dye says, 'I think I'll pull for the paycheck.' Nancy replies, 'You know, I think that's a good idea!'"

Over the years, Campbell has continued to attend the Auburn-Georgia contest, even befriending former opponents. In 2014, Lastinger invited Randy and Nancy to park at his daughter's condo in Athens and walk to Sanford Stadium. The former quarterbacks (who went 1-1 against each other as starters) had a beverage while reminiscing on 1982 and 1983.

"Those were two absolutely great games," Campbell said. "Both came down to the final play."

Inside the Rivalry

For Vince Dooley, there was no tougher task than facing Florida and Auburn in consecutive weeks. Only seven times in Dooley's twenty-five seasons did he defeat both teams the same year. In six of those seven years, his team won the conference championships. (The lone exception was 1975.) For Dooley and UGA, no year proved more challenging than 1983.

Seven days before facing Auburn, UGA had extended its conference win streak to twenty-three games with a 10–9 victory over Florida in Jacksonville. But after forty-eight months without an SEC loss, the emotional toll began to wear on Georgia.

"The toughest situation I faced every year was playing Florida and Auburn back-to-back with no off week in between," Dooley said. "I think Pat Dye put it best when he said, 'The Georgia fans won't let Georgia players come down from beating Florida to get ready for Auburn.'"

UGA quarterback John Lastinger is quick to admit that his team got outplayed by Auburn on November 12, 1983. But the slugfest a week prior didn't help. "We expended an awful lot of energy in Jacksonville," Lastinger said. "You couple that with the fact Auburn had a really good football team and it wasn't a good combination."

Following the loss to Auburn, Lastinger recalls a sense of exhaustion as he entered the locker room at Sanford Stadium. "We were tired—just physically and emotionally drained," Lastinger said.

Certainly disappointed too, but very tired. In the locker room, I just remember feeling like we'd let previous teams down. I thought, "Wow, I'm on the team that lost the conference championship." That was very hard. We felt like we left everything out there but you really have to give credit to Auburn. They were a great football team. Auburn had been knocking on the door and it was finally their time to open it.

UGA running back Keith Montgomery gets tackled by Gerald Robinson during Auburn's 1983 victory in Athens. *Morris Communications.*

Prior to facing Auburn in 1983, Georgia posted a sign in its locker room that read "GRAND SLAM." The baseball term was used as a reference for Georgia's shot at winning a fourth straight SEC title. In the end, Auburn held UGA to a triple. Still, even after the loss, Georgia could have shared the conference title if Alabama had beaten Auburn.

Sitting at his locker after the loss, a reporter asked Lastinger which team he wanted to win the Iron Bowl. Surprisingly, he said Auburn. When reminded that he would share the SEC title if Alabama won, the Valdosta, Georgia native uttered four words. "It wouldn't feel right."

II

NO. 7. AUBURN CLINGS TO VICTORY

NOVEMBER 16, 1957, AUBURN 6, GEORGIA 0

Zeke [Smith] *came to me and said, "Don't worry about it Lloyd, I'll get it right back." And that's exactly what he did.*
—*Lloyd Nix, Auburn quarterback, 1957*

CHAMPIONS

Auburn had many close calls en route to becoming 1957 national champions. They beat Florida, 13–0, Tennessee, 7–0, Kentucky, 6–0 and Georgia Tech, 3–0. No contest, however, was more gut-wrenching than the one against Georgia, who came within three yards of spoiling a perfect season.

NIX NAMED QUARTERBACK

Before November 16, 1957, there was September 1957, the month Lloyd Nix returned to Auburn from his summer job at a Birmingham steel mill. Before the era of off-season workouts, college athletes often had summer jobs before departing for school in the first week of September. The moment Nix—a rising junior—returned to Auburn, head coach Ralph "Shug" Jordan requested a meeting with his back-up halfback.

ALABAMA POLYTECHNIC INSTITUTE

AUBURN, ALABAMA

August 3, 1957

RFD 3, Box 68
Greensboro, Alabama

Dear Pat:

I hope you have had a pleasant summer. It is hard to realize that a few weeks from now we open our season against Tennessee. It stands to reason that a squad that comes back in good physical shape has a much better chance than one that comes back not ready for the strenuous type of exercise that fine football demands. So begin now, if you have not already done so, some running, shoulder and neck exercises and starts from your stance. Be sure to start out slowly in your workouts and build up the tempo as you go along. In this way you may avoid things like pulled muscles, etc.

I am asking you to report to Auburn during the afternoon of August 30. Our first meal on the training table will be that night. We can then get physical examinations and issuance of equipment out of the way and be ready to go on September 1.

If you are smoking and indulging in other things that are not good for an athlete "STOP NOW" and training will be much easier.

We have established a fine record at Auburn in recent years but I am not satisfied. I believe that we have the potential to do even better. So it will call for you and each coach to pay the greatest price ever to accomplish this.

I want you to know that we are counting on each of you to help Auburn have a successful season and the entire coaching staff joins me in sending our very best regards.

Sincerely,

Ralph Jordan
Head Football Coach

RJ:ef

Auburn coach Shug Jordan sent this letter to every player prior to the 1957 football season. *Auburn University Library Special Collections.*

"I had no idea what Coach Jordan wanted," Nix admitted. "And I definitely didn't expect him to tell me what he did." Jordan's news: Nix was his new starting quarterback. In a story that would have likely trended for days on social media, two projected starters for Auburn had been dismissed after allegedly taking items from a female dormitory. On the Plains, the incident is referred to as the panty raid that forever changed the course of Auburn history.

Okay, no one at Auburn University says that; but if they did, it wouldn't be a fabrication. To be fair to the dismissed Tigers, dorm-room raids weren't uncommon in the mid-1950s. Following World War II, the number of female students increased at many southern schools, leaving college boys with more opportunities to be, well, college boys. Throughout the 1950s, universities such as Maryland, Princeton, Washington and Nebraska had panty raids that made newspaper headlines, but none played a larger role in college football than the incident at Auburn. In a 1957 news release, Auburn officials stated that the two players were released from the team for scholastic and disciplinary reasons. "Coach Jordan told me, 'Lloyd, we've dismissed our quarterback and fullback and I want you to take over as quarterback,'" Nix said. "That decision changed my life. Athletically, it's the greatest thing that ever happened to me."

Nix was a star high school quarterback in Carbon Hill, Alabama, so he was familiar with the position. And after two years in Auburn's backfield, he understood Jordan's offensive system. Still, the signal-caller will be the first to admit that it wasn't his quarterbacking that led Auburn to the heights of college football in 1957.

"Our defense was the difference," Nix said. "I can't even explain how incredible our defense was. We gave up twenty-eight points all year."

Added All-American center Jackie Burkett: "We allowed twenty-eight points but one of those touchdowns came on an interception Lloyd threw against Houston. So we really allowed twenty-one points in ten games. If that's not an all-time record, I don't know what is."

Entering the Deep South's Oldest Rivalry, Auburn—which hadn't lost to Georgia since 1952—boasted a 7-0 record and had yielded a total of seven points to five Southeastern Conference opponents. Auburn's defense was leading the nation in points per game, total yards allowed per game and rushing yards allowed per game. On the other hand, league teams had scored sixty-five points on the Bulldogs (2-6 overall), and few gave Wallace Butts's team a chance in Columbus. However, inside Georgia's locker room at Memorial Stadium, Butts made an emotional plea to his players. About an hour before kickoff, UGA sent a telegram to Georgia Baptist Hospital in Atlanta, where General William Alexander Cunningham, UGA head coach from 1910 to 1919, was critically ill. In the telegram, Georgia players promised Cunningham they would defeat Auburn in his honor.

"We weren't a better team than Auburn," said former UGA lineman Nat Dye, older brother of Pat Dye. "But we were better than Auburn that day. We played better and did everything asked of us except win the ballgame."

Despite being favored by fourteen and a half points, Auburn struggled on offense all afternoon, scoring just one touchdown on a jump-pass from Nix to Jimmy "Red" Phillips fifty-eight seconds before halftime. Early in the third quarter, star halfback Tommy Lorino made an uncharacteristic mistake by fumbling deep in Auburn territory. After Lorino's fumble, UGA attempted four straight passes before ultimately turning the ball over on downs. One play after Auburn regained possession, Nix delivered a poor pitch to Lorino, and Georgia again recovered. Following the second fumble, Auburn sophomore Roger Duane "Zeke" Smith approached his quarterback with a guarantee.

"Zeke came to me and said, 'Don't worry about it Lloyd, I'll get it right back,'" Nix remembered. "And that's exactly what he did."

Starting on Auburn's fourteen-yard line, Georgia gained a first down, charging its way to the three. However, with the Tigers one play from a possible championship-ending setback, Smith came through on his promise. Lined up at nose guard, the future All-American was positioned next to Auburn captain Tim Baker. As the ball was snapped, Baker darted through Georgia's protection and struck quarterback Charley Britt as he tried handing off to Theron Sapp. The ball went squirming, and Smith recovered on the five-yard line. In ten games in 1957, Auburn's defense never allowed a rushing touchdown.

The morning after the nail-biting contest, a reporter from the *Columbus Enquirer* printed that Britt's hand could be seen shaking before he received the fateful snap—a claim Britt vehemently denied in September 2015.

"That's baloney!" said Britt, looking back on his fumble. "Complete baloney. I wasn't nervous at all. [Baker] just came through and knocked the ball loose. I've played a lot of football in my life and once the game got going my nerves always went away."

Adding to the excitement of Auburn's narrow 6–0 escape, both Oklahoma and Texas A&M were upset on November 16, leaving the Tigers as the lone top-ten team without a blemish. After defeating Georgia, Auburn concluded its first perfect season since 1913 by routing Florida State, 29–7, and then Alabama, 40–0. Although the Tigers were on bowl probation for paying $500 to twin recruits Robert and Harry Beaube, the Associated Press still awarded Auburn the national title.

"The funny thing is we never talked about being national champions until right before the Alabama game," Nix said. "That's when Coach Jordan

A Christmas card from Auburn's athletic department after the Tigers were crowned national champions in 1957. *Auburn University Library Special Collections.*

said, 'Men, if you play great today, you have a shot to become national champions.' Before that it was never even a thought."

For Nix, as memorable as the 1957 season was, it's his September meeting with Jordan that remains etched in the quarterback's mind. "All these years later, I still think back to being called into Coach Jordan's office that first week of September," Nix said. "This is just my opinion but I really believe [assistant] Coach [Joel] Eaves was the one who told Coach Jordan that I could play quarterback. When I signed with Auburn out of high school, Coach Jordan apparently told people he wasn't ready to have a left-handed quarterback, but I'm sure thankful he changed his mind."

Nix never lost in two years as Auburn's starter, posting a 19-0-1 record. After graduation, he went to dental school and later started a practice in Decatur, Alabama, where he worked for thirty-five years until retiring in 1999. Still, in his years since leaving Auburn, there's one game Nix always makes a point to attend.

"Whether it's in Auburn or Athens, I've been to just about every Auburn-Georgia game for forty years," Nix said in July 2015. "In fact, I've only missed one, and that's because the weather was so bad our flight to Georgia got canceled."

BAKER'S BLITZ

The morning after Auburn's 6–0 victory, newspapers throughout the South incorrectly printed that Zeke Smith caused Charley Britt to fumble near the goal line. However, after reviewing game film, it became clear that Baker caused the fumble, while Smith pounced on the loose ball. Media outlets later retracted the mistake and gave credit where it was deserved.

"It didn't bother me one bit," Baker said. "I never cared about that stuff—I just wanted to win the ballgame."

Baker, Auburn's captain in 1957, was in charge of calling defensive alignments. Well, after Auburn's second fumble (which Georgia advanced to the three-yard line), Baker signaled for Auburn's defense to set up in a six-man front. "Look, Georgia was about to score and win the ballgame," Baker said. "So I called for us to play a six-man line because that set was easiest for me. In a five-man line, I was face-to-face with the tackle, but with a six-man line, I set up right between Georgia's center and guard. I preferred being in that gap."

As Britt received the snap, he was instantly met by a charging Baker, who played right guard.

"[Britt] received the ball under center and stepped to his left," Baker recalled. "When he stepped left, I charged the gap between center and guard and wrapped my arms around him. [Britt] had the ball in both hands, but I knocked it loose before he handed off. Zeke got it."

If not for Baker's formation of six defensive linemen, it's possible, if not likely, that Georgia would have spoiled Auburn's chance at a national championship.

"Like I said, the only reason I called a six-man front was because it was easiest for me," said Baker, laughing. "We got tired during ballgames, so I wanted to call defenses that would help me out. Sometimes I'd call a five-four or a five-three, but I happened to call a six-man front on that play against Georgia."

WHAT MIGHT HAVE BEEN

Sitting inside Frederica House Restaurant on St. Simons Island, Jimmy Orr held a vodka-cranberry cocktail in his right hand while separating his left thumb and index finger three inches apart. "Charley [Britt] overthrew me by this much," said Orr, who led the SEC in receiving in 1957. Orr is best known for his thirteen-year career in the National Football League, including a Super Bowl V victory with the Baltimore Colts. However, on a warm March night in 2016, the eighty-year-old spent time reflecting on the 1957 edition of the Deep South's Oldest Rivalry.

"Back in those days, everyone played both ways," said Orr, a senior at UGA in 1957. "I was our punter, too. Well, the week before we played Auburn, our coaches kept warning me about [Auburn end Jerry] Wilson and how great he was at blocking punts."

Georgia received the opening kickoff, and Orr (who also returned kicks) took Billy Atkins's boot from UGA's five to the twenty-six. Georgia gained eight yards in three plays before Orr dropped back to punt at his own thirty-four. "I get ready to kick," Orr said, "and all I'm doing is looking over at Wilson on the end. I was so focused on not letting him block the kick that I completely shanked the thing."

Orr's punt went six yards—from Georgia's thirty-four to the forty—before landing out of bounds near the Little Roundman.

"Coach Butts was so mad. He took off his hat and threw it down right by the football," Orr said. "That was the only time I was thankful to play both way."

Despite Orr's miscue, Georgia's defense held strong and forced Auburn to turn the ball over on downs. Orr's punting, however, eventually proved costly. With a scoreless game late in the second quarter, the Seneca, South Carolina native struck another below-average kick. The ball sailed twenty-seven yards and landed at Auburn's forty-eight. Taking advantage of the field position, Lloyd Nix and Red Phillips finished the fifty-two-yard drive by connecting on a four-yard touchdown—the lone score of the game. Still, despite being two-touchdown underdogs, Georgia had a chance to tie the contest early in the third quarter. After UGA's offense failed to cross midfield in the first half, Georgia tackle Riley Gunnels recovered a Tommy Lorino fumble on Auburn's ten-yard line just two minutes into the third quarter. On UGA's first play, Britt targeted his go-to receiver in the end zone. "Three inches," Orr said. "The ball was three inches out of my reach or we would've tied that ballgame."

Britt attempted three more passes after missing Orr, but UGA failed to gain a first down. "Auburn was a very, very good football team in 1957," Orr said. "Unbelievable defense."

Orr shook his head, gently put down his cocktail and began eating his favorite meal at Frederica House: baked chicken with two sides of cheese grits. He was done talking about the 6–0 loss in Columbus. He wasn't through, however, reminiscing on his time in Athens. Orr fell in love with Georgia on October 19, 1946, fifteen days after his tenth birthday. In honor of turning double digits, Orr's father, a doctor in Seneca, asked his son how he wanted to celebrate. "I said, 'I want to go watch [Charley] Trippi play,'" Orr recalled. "So my dad took me to the Oklahoma A&M game, and I fell in love with Georgia."

As he dipped each bite of chicken into grits, Orr's mind traveled from 1946 to the summer of 1957, only months after suffering a career-threatening knee injury during his junior season. "Hardly anyone gave me a chance to play my senior year at Georgia," Orr said. "In the summer of '57, I went to Camp Carolina where I worked as a counselor and took a knee machine with me. I ran those hills all summer and it got me back in shape."

One night after work, the rising senior drove to Highlands, North Carolina, which Orr called "my hangout spot," and spotted a Cadillac parked near the Highlands auction house. "I knew immediately that Cadillac belonged to Coach Butts," Orr said. Like most Georgia players, Orr had his share of arguments with Butts throughout the mid-1950s. The disciplinary coach asked Orr, a former walk-on, to leave practice on two occasions, while the receiver briefly quit the team once and drove home to Seneca.

"I got to Seneca and thought, 'Boy I've really made a mistake. I hope they call me,'" Orr said. "Dan Magill [UGA's sports information director] called and said, 'Come on back.'"

However, despite the occasional disagreement, Orr and Butts maintained a strong relationship, and the senior wanted to see his coach in Highlands. "I waited outside the auction house till he came out, and sure enough, he and his wife, Winnie, and another couple eventually appeared," Orr said. "Coach Butts and I shook hands and talked while the other three started walking off. Well, we're walking about five yards behind them and Coach Butts fumbles around his pockets and comes up with twenty dollars to give to me. Then, we walk about ten more yards and he calls the other man back and told that man to give me ten dollars more. You know, that was probably illegal, but it showed me he looked after his players. Coach Butts was harder than you'd ever imagine, but deep down he really did care."

BECOMING NATIONAL CHAMPIONS

Sure, Auburn players and coaches deserve credit for going 10-0, but the Tigers may not have earned a national championship if it wasn't for Bill Beckwith, Auburn's sports information director. As the 1957 season crept into November, the Tigers were climbing the Associated Press poll—which crowned its national champion before bowl games—but remained close in votes with one-loss Ohio State. That changed, however, when Beckwith discovered that every radio station with an AP outlet was allowed to cast a vote. Prior to playing against Alabama on November 30, Beckwith contacted numerous stations throughout the South (who didn't realize they had a vote) and wrote them all a specific letter. A plea on November 27, 1957, to radio station WPBB in Jackson, Alabama, read:

> *Dear Mr. McCorquodale,*
> *Auburn's football team can finish as the nation's No. 1 team with your help. Radio Station WPBB in your town can vote but we need you to inform them, or to vote for them with their permission Saturday night or Sunday. Enclosed is a complete instruction sheet. Please keep this confidential.*
> *Thanks and WAR EAGLE.*

Sincerely yours,
Bill Beckwith

Hundreds of similar letters were sent to media outlets in Alabama, Georgia, Tennessee, Louisiana and Mississippi. In the end, the strategy remained a secret, and Auburn ran away with the national title. According to Paul Hemphill's book *Lost in the Lights*, the people at Ohio State never knew what hit them. The votes for Auburn began rolling in at the Associated Press headquarters at Rockefeller Center in New York in such an avalanche that the AP sports editor, Ted Smits, phoned Beckwith around dark that evening. "Call 'em off, Bill," he said. "You've won the national championship." The AP formed a panel of voters soon after the 1957 season.

After the rankings were finalized, Beckwith sent thank-you notes to every station that voted. A letter to W.A. Brown of Ozark, Alabama, stated:

Dear Mr. Brown,
Now that the smoke has cleared and the skies are clear and sunny, I'd like to express the appreciation of the Auburn Athletic Department and myself for the help you rendered during our little No. 1 campaign.
As you know, we would probably have won without the little promotion, but we like the way the votes rolled in.
Again, thanks from us and the nation's No. 1 football team.
Sincerely,
Bill Beckwith

NO. 8. WATER UNLEASHED AT JORDAN-HARE

NOVEMBER 15, 1986, GEORGIA 20, AUBURN 16

The Monday after the game I was scheduled to speak at a turf conference at the University of Georgia, so I went to Coach Dye and asked if he thought I should cancel. Knowing Coach Dye, he made it very clear what I should do. He said, "Tell those Georgia students that dogs need a bath once-and-awhile anyway."
—*Paul Conner, who opened the sprinkler valve on UGA fans in 1986.*

Inside Paul Conner's Auburn home is a football signed by members of the Tigers 1986 coaching staff. The ball was never used in a game or touched by an Auburn player. But for Conner, born 1929 in Guntersville, Alabama, it's one of his proudest keepsakes.

"The ball was presented to me after George Toma, the famous NFL groundskeeper for Super Bowls, awarded Auburn for having the best field in college football," Conner said. "We were so proud of that accomplishment. We were so proud of our field."

Conner worked in Auburn's engineering department for two decades before shifting to athletics in the early 1980s. At that point, he was asked by newly hired football coach Pat Dye to redesign Auburn's field. It was a costly project, one that Auburn didn't immediately have funds for.

"But we eventually made it happen," Conner said.

With the level of investment in the field, Conner and Auburn University officials began discussing what actions should transpire if fans ever decided to rush the terrain. Throughout the mid-1980s, Conner and administrators had multiple meetings before a rule was made: If fans come on the field, turn on the sprinkler valve.

"There were two reasons behind our decision," Conner said. "First, we didn't want anyone getting hurt. Second, we needed to protect our field."

On November 15, 1986, Conner was called into action. But first, before water flowed, there was a game—a game that Dooley's Dogs, as ten-and-a-half-point underdogs, had seemingly little chance of winning. Georgia entered the contest with a 6-3 record, unranked and injured. Tailbacks Tim Worley and Keith Henderson were both sidelined with knee injuries. Uga IV, Georgia's mascot, even hurt his knee while jumping from a hotel bed before the Vanderbilt game. In addition to being plagued by misfortune, Georgia arrived in Auburn unsure who their quarterback would be. James Jackson, who started the first nine games of 1986, had left Athens early in the week to attend his grandmother's funeral in Camilla, Georgia.

"James went home after Monday's practice and he told me he probably wouldn't make it to Auburn," said Wayne Johnson, UGA's backup. "James was very, very close to his grandmother. She was like a mother to him."

Despite suggesting to Johnson he wouldn't play, Jackson never gave Dooley that indication. In fact, the night before kickoff, Dooley believed Jackson would be his signal caller.

"James and I roomed together for away games," Johnson said. "Each trip, Coach Dooley would knock on everyone's door to see if we wanted juice or a snack before bed. Well, the night before Auburn, we were staying at the Ramada Inn in LaGrange and Coach Dooley came and knocked on the door. Coach Dooley said, 'Wayne, be on the lookout for James. He's supposed to come back tonight.'"

The night passed, and Jackson never showed. On Saturday morning, Dooley phoned Johnson's hotel room, asking if his roommate had arrived.

"I said, 'No sir,'" Johnson recalled.

So Dooley started Johnson, a redshirt sophomore who had thrown four passes all season. The decision caught many by surprise, including members of Johnson's family, who made the short drive from Columbus to Auburn. Also taken aback was ESPN. "Moments before the game, ESPN was still talking about James Jackson being our starter," Johnson said. "When they found out it was me, I had to run get my headshot taken outside the dressing room for TV."

As hectic as the pregame was, Johnson was poised under the bright lights of Jordan-Hare Stadium. He threw for a touchdown, ran for another and surged his Bulldogs ahead, 20-10, with less than five minutes to play.

However, as Georgia's upset neared completion, No. 8 Auburn stormed back. Sparked by the arm of junior quarterback Jeff Burger, Auburn marched ninety-eight yards to cut its deficit to 20–16 with 2:51 remaining. Then, after forcing a UGA punt, Burger had an opportunity to keep his team in the hunt for an SEC championship.

As the clock ticked below one minute, Auburn had already gone from its own six to Georgia's forty-five-yard line when offensive coordinator Pat Sullivan signaled for Burger to call play "82." With his excitement overflowing, Burger misread Sullivan's call and instead told his team to execute "92."

"I lost my composure," Burger said. "There's no other way to put it. If I would've called 82, Georgia was in a two-high defense and we had a seam route going straight down the middle. That seam route would have been there."

Instead, 92 played into Georgia's alignment, and Burger's pass was intercepted by linebacker Steve Boswell. Just like that, the Tigers were eliminated from SEC title contention. "That interception hurt me so bad," said Burger, a native of Cedartown, Georgia. "We were moving right down the field until I called the wrong play. You know, I will say this, though: I grew up as a football player after that loss."

For Georgia's 1986 senior class, it was their first victory over Auburn, and the same was true for many Bulldog students. As Dooley was being interviewed by ESPN's Tim Brando, a number of UGA fans left their seats and made their way onto Auburn's field. Some stayed in the end zone. Others ventured to midfield and began ripping away pieces of Auburn's logo.

"That's when I got a call from our press box to turn on the main sprinkler valve," Conner said. "But I want to make one thing clear. Over the years, I've heard people say we sprayed Georgia fans with fire hoses or water cannons. That simply isn't true. We turned on all six sprinklers and they didn't have nearly enough pressure to hurt people. Georgia fans were taking our turf and we wanted to get them away."

Ironically, the man who ordered Conner to unleash the water was Auburn's assistant athletic director for facilities, Kermit Perry, a 1955 graduate of the University of Georgia. Decades have come and gone, but 1986 continues to be a bitter topic for some alumni. Auburn folks are upset that opposing fans rushed their field. Georgia supporters are unhappy that Conner and Perry resorted to sprinklers, soaking fans on a chilly November night, including many who had remained in the stands all along.

"I definitely thought it was wrong to spray water," Johnson said. "The year before, I still remember Auburn tearing up our hedges. Our fans just wanted to have fun, too."

Renowned author Lewis Grizzard wrote in a column for the *Atlanta Constitution*: "If you're at somebody else's house and they ask you not to wear your shoes on their carpet, as overly fastidious as that might be, in a polite society you don't do it. But if you do, all you deserve is a polite reprimand, not a slap in the face."

Sonny Seiler, owner of Georgia's mascot, Uga, disagreed with both Johnson and Grizzard. "What's there to be upset about? We won the ballgame! To be honest, I thought the whole thing was sort of funny."

Still, the controversy was viewed as a black eye by Auburn University president James E. Martin. In a written statement, Martin explained, "We regret such an unfortunate incident has occurred on the Auburn campus. This is not the type of behavior or response we associate with the Auburn community." The Monday after the game, Martin appointed an ad hoc committee to make recommendations on how Auburn could better handle crowd control. The committee (made up of Auburn's Dr. George Emert, Dr. Pat Barnes, Dr. Joe Boland, Dr. Dennis Rygiel, Hindman Wall and Student Government Association president Robert Maund) met on November 18, December 2 and January 23. After the third meeting, the committee finalized a fifteen-point plan to ensure that the sprinkler incident wouldn't occur again. The first of the fifteen points said that tickets for all Auburn football games should include wording that allows reasonable searches for alcoholic beverages. No. 4 stated that only professional security forces should be used for crowd control during athletic events. No. 11 noted that careful consideration should be given to which games are played at night.

As for Conner, decades later, he never imagined his field would remain in the minds of so many. "It's crazy how many people remember that moment," Conner said. "People still talk about it all the time. When I turned on those sprinklers, I had no idea it would be remembered thirty years later."

FULLWOOD'S TOUCHDOWN THAT WASN'T

As much as the sprinkler incident is remembered by fans, running back Brent Fullwood has another memory. On Auburn's first possession of the second half, the Kissimmee, Florida native took Burger's handoff and searched for a hole off left tackle. Almost instantly, he was met by three Georgia defenders and the play seemed destined for a loss. Instead, Fullwood escaped and darted twenty-five yards to the end zone.

"In my mind, it's a touchdown," said Fullwood, who finished sixth in the 1986 Heisman Trophy voting. "I know Georgia never stopped me."

But as Fullwood sprinted into the open field, a sideline official whistled the play dead.

"They claimed my forward momentum had stopped," Fullwood said.

It wasn't right and it still isn't right. I'm a running back. Sometimes they stop you and you go sideways. You go backwards. You go forwards. That's what running backs do, but I was nowhere near being tackled on that play. When those officials blew the whistle that was a huge momentum lift for Georgia.

Auburn trailed 13–7 at the time, and Fullwood's score would have evened the contest, giving the Tigers a chance to recapture the lead pending a Chris Knapp extra point. Instead, Knapp made a forty-one-yard field goal to cut Georgia's led to 13–10. Auburn never got any closer. "Out of every play of my career, that one hurts the most," Fullwood said. "No doubt about it. I know officials have to make judgment calls and they aren't always easy to do. Still, in my heart, I know I scored. I know that was a touchdown."

As stunned as Fullwood was about the whistle, so were ESPN announcers Mike Patrick and Pat McInally.

"He's too good for the game," McInally blared over the ESPN airwaves. "That's definitely a bad whistle by the officials....They just aren't accustomed to human beings being able to take this many hits and stay upright."

Boswell Seals Victory

Like so many prized recruits from the Peach State, Steve Boswell's college decision came down to Auburn and Georgia. As a native of Warner Robins, Georgia, the linebacker wanted to remain in his home state, but there was considerable pressure from Auburn defensive coordinator Frank Orgel. Orgel, who played alongside Pat Dye on UGA's 1959 conference championship team, was hired by his former teammate at Auburn in 1981. However, before coming to the Plains, Orgel coached Warner Robins High School from 1970 to 1972, leading the school to a 28-4-2 record.

"Orgel coached my older brother at Warner Robins," Boswell said. "I used to sit on his lap and watch game film on Saturday mornings. Man, I'm not joking—the hardest thing I ever had to do was tell Frank Orgel I wasn't coming to Auburn."

Boswell signed with Georgia in 1983, but he never forgot how close of a decision it was between the Tigers and Bulldogs. "Every player has that one game they want to win most," Boswell said. "Mine was Auburn. I wanted to prove to Coach Orgel that I could play."

During his first three seasons in Athens, Boswell and the rest of his signing class went 0-3 in the Deep South's Oldest Rivalry, including a 24–10 defeat in 1985 at Sanford Stadium. Adding to Boswell's displeasure, Orgel left Auburn following the 1985 season to go to South Carolina. Still, without Orgel on the opposing sideline, without quarterback James Jackson, without tailbacks Tim Worley and Keith Henderson, and without a shot of winning the SEC title, Boswell delivered the play of his career in 1986 against the team he always hoped to beat.

With Auburn vying to win a conference championship, Boswell intercepted Jeff Burger with less than a minute remaining to secure the 20–16 victory. After the game, Boswell held tight to the game ball, telling teammates he would never let go. Decades later, the keepsake remains on a mantel in Boswell's childhood home in Warner Robins.

"It still has the Auburn logo on it, but my dad painted it up and put the game score, too," Boswel said in 2016. "I'm fifty-one years old and that interception is my claim to fame. Every November, I'm dragged out of the ashes and come to life again because of that one play at Auburn."

After the game, Dooley awarded Boswell a black bone for the interception, which was placed on his helmet. In four years at UGA, it was the only black bone Boswell earned.

"Back then, we had stars on our helmets for big plays, but if you made a *really* big play, Coach Dooley gave you a bone," Boswell said. "Dooley was the only person allowed to give out black bones, which was an unbelievable honor."

In addition to the bone, Boswell received a congratulatory phone call from Orgel. "I was upset he wasn't there to see it, but that phone call meant a lot," the linebacker said. "Hell, it meant everything."

As for the sprinkler incident, Boswell says neither institution should have hard feelings. In fact, he wants Auburn and Georgia to embrace the water.

"Nobody was in the wrong," Boswell said. "I thought it was the coolest thing ever they hosed us down and I thought it was the coolest thing ever our students rushed the field. Man, this is the Deep South's Oldest Rivalry. It's Georgia-Auburn. That water made the game legendary."

13

NO. 9. SINKWICH TO RACEHORSE

NOVEMBER 1, 1941, GEORGIA 7, AUBURN 0

Less than a block from the St. Simons Island pier sits a clothing shop on Mallery Street named Roberta's By the Sea. Inside, ceramic Bulldogs surround the shelves while a black-and-white photograph is hidden in the back of the store. The ancient picture shows four football players and has the inscription "Georgia's dream backfield—Frank Sinkwich, Charley Trippi, Dick McPhee, Lamar 'Racehorse' Davis."

Davis, who passed away in 2008, owned Roberta's, which he named for his daughter. And even though the photograph is dated 1942, the play Davis is best known for occurred a season before on November 1, 1941.

Lamar "Racehorse" Davis (*far right*) is pictured with UGA greats Frank Sinkwich (*far left*), Charley Trippi and Dick McPhee. *UGA Athletic Department.*

On a sunny afternoon at Memorial Stadium, Auburn and Georgia had battled to a 0–0 deadlock late in the fourth quarter. With Auburn unwilling to punt toward Davis, Monk Gafford's kick sailed out of bounds at Georgia's thirty-six-yard line with three seconds remaining. Needing sixty-four yards on the final play, nearly every spectator assumed the sixth tie between Auburn and Georgia was in order. But what ensued was the play that sent UGA to the Orange Bowl—its first postseason appearance in school history.

Starting at his thirty-six-yard line, junior Frankie Sinkwich called the play "pass two-ends in front" and heaved a forty-yard pass in the direction of Racehorse Davis. With Auburn's Gafford and Aubrey Clayton defending, Davis hauled in the reception, then darted twenty-four yards untouched for the miraculous score. On the front page of the *Athens Banner-Herald*, an article proclaimed, "Georgia seemed not to have a ghost of a chance, but the ghost walked into Memorial Stadium before some 17,000 customers."

Before the final play, Sinkwich had completed just three of fifteen passes for twenty-five yards. However, all that mattered was the final Hail Mary, which went in the record books for sixty-four yards and a touchdown. After Davis crossed the goal line, placekicker Leo Costa converted the unnecessary extra point, upping the final score to 7–0.

Following the 1941 victory, UGA students repeatedly sang Georgia's popular fight song, "I Want to Go Back." Its lyrics are as follows:

I want to go back to U.G.A.
Back to dear ole Athens town
Back to where I spend my check
Back to where it's "To hell with Tech"
Want to go back to U.G.A.
Back to dear ole Athens town
Want-a go back, got-a go back
To U.G., U.G., G-E-O-R-G-I-A!

Auburn, which had suffered three defeats before facing one-loss UGA, entered the 1941 contest as thirteen-point underdogs, which made the Hail Mary even more demoralizing. An article by Stuart Stephenson of the *Montgomery Advertiser* stated: "Auburn faithful followed their favorites, thrice beaten, into this glorious November Saturday and watched spellbound and popeyed as the Tigers virtually stopped one of the greatest offensive backs, Frankie Sinkwich. These faithful saw an unexpected drama of the gridiron unfold before their unbelieving eyes. They saw a Tiger team reach its loftiest peak of the season—only to lose the 46th game of the long and brilliant series on the very last play."

When the contest ended, UGA players embraced Davis and Sinkwich, while Ears Whitworth, Georgia's line coach, could be seen giving Davis a well-earned kiss. An article written by Johnny Bradberry, assistant sports editor of the *Atlanta Journal*, proclaimed:

> *Fans sat stunned in their seats as Auburn players pinched themselves to see if it was real. Georgia players swarmed on the field to congratulate Sinkwich and Davis. But Ears Whitworth, the line coach, was there first. He gave them a bear hug which would make Gargantua ashamed of himself. He even went so far as to kiss Davis. Sinkwich escaped [a kiss] with his best run of the day—a sterling 75-yard sprint to the dressing room.*

Ignited by Davis's score, Georgia's 1941 squad posted a 9-1-1 record, capped off by a 40–26 victory over Texas Christian University in the Orange Bowl. After playing professionally for the Baltimore Colts, Davis returned to St. Simons Island, where he had been raised as a child. For decades, he worked for Rich Seapak Corporation before later opening Roberta's By the Sea. In 1990, Davis was inducted into the Georgia Sports Hall of Fame.

14

NO. 10. THE MIRACLE ON THE PLAINS

NOVEMBER 16, 1996, GEORGIA 56, AUBURN 49

The ballgame was over. It was. All Auburn had to do was go celebrate on their sideline and they win. There's no way we could've killed the clock if [Charles Dorsey] *didn't do what he did.*
—UGA quarterback Mike Bobo

Halfway down a winding Savannah neighborhood, Sonny Seiler—who received a certain pure white English bulldog for a wedding gift in 1956—sits in his home surrounded by memorabilia. Above his couch is the first college jersey Herschel Walker ever wore. Beside a lamp are mementos from his mascot lineage: From Uga I's original outfit to Uga IV posing in New York at the 1982 Heisman Trophy presentation. Finally, above Seiler's favorite chair is a photograph of his son, Charles, tugging a leash as Uga V leaps in the direction of Auburn receiver Robert Baker.

"You can see the dog was jumping toward Baker's forearm," Seiler said. "At that point, Charles jerked back on him but not before a young lady photographer [Patricia Miklik] from the *Montgomery Advertiser* captured this photo."

Miklik's image became an instant sensation with Georgia fans throughout the country. Also requesting prints were magazines, newspapers and more than a handful of Alabama supporters. Although Seiler's mascots had long been prize possessions of the University of Georgia, the photograph turned Uga V into a national celebrity, eventually landing him on the cover of *Sports Illustrated*.

Todd Donnan (*right*) embraces his father after UGA's victory at Jordan-Hare Stadium. *Morris Communications*.

"The *Montgomery Advertiser* sold so many copies that the original negative wore out," Seiler said. "Can you believe that? The picture was in everything."

Seiler wasn't exaggerating. The original negative indeed wore out. In the weeks after Uga V attempted to bite Baker, Seiler watched as his dog captured the heart of Bulldog Nation. Then, shortly before Christmas in 1996, he received a call originating from an Alabama area code.

"Sure enough, it was the young lady who snapped the photo," Seiler said. "She introduced herself and I said, 'I thought you would've retired by now from all the money you've made off this photo.' She said, 'Oh, Mr. Seiler, I didn't make a nickel. I was salaried by the paper and they got it all.'"

Before hanging up, Miklik asked Seiler for a favor. "She said, 'Mr. Seiler, if I send a few copies will you sign them for me?'" Seiler recalled. "I said, 'Sure, I'll sign them for you if you also send me two copies. I want one and I want Charles to have one.' So that's exactly what she did."

Although Seiler can reminisce with levity on the bite attempt heard 'round college football, it was no laughing matter on November 16, 1996. The moment after it happened, Charles found his father and professed that he and Uga V had never left their designated area.

"People don't understand how difficult it is bringing a dog to another stadium," Seiler said. "A whole lot goes into it. More than most will ever realize."

INSIDE THE RIVALRY

Robert Cedrick Baker III never played for Auburn University after 1996. The standout receiver was declared academically ineligible before the 1997 season, had a brief NFL stint with the Miami Dolphins and then became involved in drug trafficking.

In May 1998, Baker, twenty-two at the time, pled guilty in Opelika, Alabama, to cocaine trafficking and was sentenced to fifteen years in prison. His term was cut significantly short when Baker helped lead officers to the arrests of three others in the case. Baker was again pulled over on January 20, 2013, in Valdosta, Georgia, on a traffic violation. Lowndes County deputies searched his vehicle and found 59.5 grams of heroin and a nine-millimeter semiautomatic pistol.

"Mr. Baker made a terrible mistake when he chose to traffic illegal drugs, and particularly when he brought a gun along to help him do so," Michael Moore, the U.S. attorney for the Middle District of Georgia, said in a press release. "He will have a long time to reflect on that mistake in federal prison."

Since 2014, Baker has been incarcerated at FPC Pensacola, a minimum security federal prison camp with 726 male offenders. The former receiver, whose image hangs on the walls of countless UGA homes and businesses, is known as inmate No. 96761-020.

Baker's release date is July 19, 2018.

The Game

"Uga V vs. Robert Baker" occurred after Auburn's first score. Fourteen touchdowns later, Georgia had pulled off a stunner. Looking back, the 100th playing of the Deep South's Oldest Rivalry may have been UGA's most unexpected victory. Auburn had SEC title dreams and a 7-2 record. Georgia had a first-year head coach in Jim Donnan, a 3-5 record, and leading up to the game, UGA elected to bench quarterback Mike Bobo and running back Robert Edwards.

"We hadn't had a lot of offensive chemistry going into the Auburn game, so we decided to start Smitty [Brian Smith] at quarterback," Donnan said. "We needed to try something different."

By his own admission, the game still lingers in the mind of Auburn quarterback Dameyune Craig. For UGA offensive lineman Matt Stinchcomb, it's the contest he remembers most from his career in Athens. Stinchcomb, a sophomore, had already seen his team fall to Southern Miss, South Carolina, Tennessee, Kentucky and Florida. He admitted, "It would have been easy for us to lose again."

"We weren't even bowl eligible at the end of the year," said Stinchcomb, whose girlfriend, now wife, was an Auburn student in 1996. "On top of everything, our starting quarterback and starting tailback had just been benched. So, yeah, we had plenty of reasons to lay down."

But Georgia didn't. Not after trailing 7–0 just 135 seconds into the first quarter. Not after trailing 28–7 with 6:07 remaining before halftime (at which point Bobo entered the game, replacing Smith). Not after trailing 28–21 with one second left in regulation. Each time, Georgia battled back, eventually prevailing in four overtimes. It was the first overtime contest in SEC history.

"Everything we talked about in the weight room, our offseason program and conditioning, it all paid off that day," Donnan said. "You're talking

Despite not starting, UGA quarterback Mike Bobo came off the bench to lead the Bulldogs to an improbable victory at Jordan-Hare Stadium. *Morris Communications*.

about one of the longest games in SEC history, and I felt like we played our best football in the fourth quarter and overtime."

Other than Uga V's leap, the defining play happened with one second remaining and Georgia needing a touchdown to force overtime. Thirty yards from Auburn's end zone, the Bulldogs called "Flex Right Slide Left 287 Corner/Wide," a play primarily designed to target Hines Ward.

"I was the last 7 and had a post corner route against defensive back Jayson Bray," wide receiver Corey Allen said.

Allen, who claims he was the third option on the play, wound up being Bobo's target.

"I initially didn't think Mike was coming my way because Hines had a clear path in the middle of the field," Allen remembered. "But when Auburn double-teamed Hines, it left me one-on-one with Jayson. Mike just threw it up and gave me a chance."

Despite catching the ball with both feet on the one-yard line, the receiver dove toward the end zone and lunged across for the first touchdown of his career. The play sent the contest to overtime, but before extra sessions, Donnan was approached by his son. At the time, Todd Donnan wasn't part of Georgia's coaching staff, but he happened to be watching from the sideline.

"Todd grew up around football his whole life," Donnan said. "He played for me at Marshall but rarely suggested anything when it came to coaching. Well, standing beside me before that first overtime at Auburn, Todd goes, 'Dad, I don't like to tell you what to do. We both know that. But I'd give Robert Edwards the ball every play during overtime.' You know, that's just about what we did."

Edwards had only six carries before overtime, but he dominated the extra sessions, scoring on runs of nine yards, five yards and nine yards. In all, Edwards had ten carries for sixty-two yards in the four overtime periods, leading Georgia to a 56–49 upset. Looking back on the game, Stinchcomb believes that not starting Edwards was key to the outcome. Not because his benching sent a message, but for the fact that he had fresh legs when it mattered.

"Strategically, look, I don't think it was intentional, but it definitely didn't hurt having Robert rested for overtime," Stinchcomb said. "Everybody else was dead tired and we had a guy who didn't have as much tear on him. That was huge."

FROM BENCHED TO HERO

In the game before facing Auburn, UGA suffered a forty-point loss to Florida, blindsiding a storied program in Athens. Through eight contests in 1996, Mike Bobo had thrown fifteen interceptions and was benched a day after returning from Jacksonville.

"We were completely embarrassed by Florida," Bobo said. "I'll be the first to admit I wasn't getting the job done."

As the son of a coach, Bobo accepted his demotion with grace, even telling Donnan that Brian Smith deserved to take his spot as captain for the Auburn game. Still, despite not receiving any first-team snaps leading up to the Deep South's Oldest Rivalry, Bobo prepared like he'd be called upon.

"One thing I was taught growing up was how to respond to adverse situations," Bobo said. "When Coach Donnan told me I wasn't starting, I said, 'Yes, sir,' but prepared all week like I might play. It's all about doing what's best for the team and you better believe I gave Brian Smith every bit of support."

It didn't take long for Donnan's experiment with Smith to turn ugly. Struggling to move on Auburn's defense, UGA trailed 28–7 before Bobo was asked to provide damage control midway through the second quarter. Suddenly, Georgia found momentum. Sparked by a fumble recovery from Champ Bailey, Bobo drove thirty-four yards and cut Auburn's halftime lead to 28–14.

"The whole time we were losing I remember Joe Kines, our defensive coordinator, pacing the sidelines," Bobo recalled. "He was telling everyone, 'Keep playing, men. One play at a time—you never know what's gonna happen. Just keep playing, men!'"

The longer UGA hung around, the more breaks began to go their way. By all accounts, Auburn dominated the third quarter, possessing the ball for eleven minutes, but wasn't able to score. One long drive ended in a fumble; another ended with an errant field goal. Then, starting the fourth period, Bobo connected with Ward for a sixty-seven-yard touchdown, trimming its deficit to 28–21.

The score went unchanged until UGA's final possession. Needing a touchdown to force overtime, Bobo drove Georgia from its own eighteen-yard line to Auburn's twenty-two in less than a minute. Then, with nineteen seconds remaining and no timeouts, Bobo dropped back and searched for an open receiver.

"I use this example every year when I'm talking to my quarterbacks," said Bobo, head coach at Colorado State University. "There's nothing more important than time when you're running a one-minute offense. You can't take a sack. No matter what, you can't take a sack. Throw it away. Get rid of the ball. Whatever you do, don't *waste* the clock."

In front of a sellout crowd at Jordan-Hare Stadium, Bobo wasted the clock. Unwilling to throw the ball away, Bobo was sacked by linebacker Marcus Washington at the thirty-yard line, likely ending the game. Donnan removed his headset in concession of defeat. Auburn began celebrating on the field. By all accounts, the game was over.

However, in a state of excitement, Auburn defensive lineman Charles Dorsey picked up the football and ran toward the fifty-yard line. Because Bobo was ruled down before the ball came loose, officials stopped the clock, which gave Georgia a chance to regroup. As the clock restarted, Bobo spiked the ball with one click remaining.

"The ballgame was over," Bobo said. "It was. All Auburn had to do was go celebrate on their sideline and they win. There's no way we could've killed the clock if [Dorsey] didn't do what he did."

Bobo finished with 360 passing yards and two touchdowns, one of which came on the last second of regulation.

IV
THE MOMENTS

UGA fullback Ronnie
Stewart (33) hugs Norris
Brown (88) after his
touchdown catch to end the
first half of the 1980 contest
at Jordan-Hare Stadium.
The Augusta Chronicle.

15

THE HARTFORD EXPRESS—1965

AUBURN 21, GEORGIA 19

Vince Dooley roamed the University of Georgia sideline from 1964 to 1989, coaching twenty-five times in the Deep South's Oldest Rivalry. What game does he remember most? Well, it's not any of the eleven wins. To Dooley's displeasure, it's a two-point defeat that occurred during his second season in Athens.

"I can't forget 1965," Dooley said. "I hate to say it, but when I think about facing Auburn, that's the first game that comes to mind....We were going in for the game-winning score and I got ahead of myself. I started to rush. Instead of taking it slow and playing to the situation, I wanted to score immediately."

Trailing 21–19 inside Auburn's five-yard line, Dooley called for a handoff from quarterback Kirby Moore to sophomore Ronnie Jenkins. Jenkins had already scored twice, but as UGA's fullback plunged toward the goal line for a third time, the ball came loose.

"I live with the memory of turning around and seeing that ball on the ground," Moore said. "That's one of the few fumbles Ronnie ever had; he was just trying to get himself braced to run over people."

Robert Fulghum recovered the fumble caused by John Cochran, helping preserve Auburn's victory in front of a disheartened crowd of 46,812. Cochran, a senior engineering student from Crossville, Alabama, also blocked an extra point and batted down a two-point conversion attempt.

"I got lucky on the goal line stand because Georgia ran to my side instead of my roommate Bill Cody's side," said Cochran, now professor emeritus for

Auburn's aerospace engineering department. "I happened to hit the football with my helmet."

Added Jenkins: "I took that loss harder than you could ever imagine. I cried like a baby. For a week after my fumble, I was still crying."

Following Auburn's win, Jack Doane, sports editor of the *Montgomery Advertiser* wrote, "All men dedicated to the proposition that Auburn must win the Southeastern Conference may now rise and bow in the direction of one John Cochran, a studious type fellow who saved the Plainsmen's hides here Saturday."

Auburn's victory over UGA kept Cochran's team in contention for a conference title. The Tigers fell short, however, losing to Alabama in its regular-season finale.

THE HARTFORD EXPRESS

Ronnie Jenkins's fumble may have sealed the outcome, but the performance by Auburn junior Tom Bryan put the Tigers in position for victory. Bryan rushed for 162 yards on nineteen carries—a solid output, especially considering he had changed positions thirteen days before facing Georgia. As a high school star from Hartford, Alabama (a small town on the Alabama-Florida line), Bryan initially committed to Paul "Bear" Bryant and Alabama, even signing paperwork to attend the Tuscaloosa school. But a lingering fear of having to change positions led Bryan to reconsider, and he eventually chose Auburn with hopes of playing quarterback.

"I didn't go to that other school because I was afraid they'd move me to running back," Bryan said. "As it turned out, Auburn eventually moved me, too."

Although Bryan ended up starring at Auburn, earning the nickname the "Hartford Express," it was difficult leaving Geneva County and having to adjust to college life. Bryan dealt with hardships growing up, including losing his father at an early age, and he was admittedly pampered by his mother throughout his teenage years.

"When I got to Auburn, I had no idea what was in store," Bryan said. "All of the sudden I was thrown in this world of freshman football and there wasn't anybody to care for me. It was dog-eat-dog. It was hot. I was getting beat up and I didn't like anything about it. I wanted some tender love and care and it was nowhere to be found."

As preseason conditioning grew tougher, Bryan walked off the field following Auburn's first September scrimmage in 1963. He was prepared to quit football and return to Hartford, when the head coach of Auburn's freshman team, Vince Dooley, gave chase.

"Coach Dooley kind of ran after me," Bryan remembered. "He said, 'Tom, where do you think you're going?' I was an immature kid and said, 'I can't do this anymore.' Coach Dooley said, 'It's tough right now but that's how it has to be. We have to get rid of some guys but we don't want to get rid of you. Tom, you need to come on back out.'"

Bryan's decision to stay was further solidified when a hometown friend called that same week.

"I kept calling my mother and telling her how bad they were treating me," Bryan said.

Finally, I got a call from a family friend who helped recruit me to Auburn. Well, come to find out, my mother had been telling him how unhappy I was. So he called and said, "Tom, your mother is worried to death about you. You need to decide if you want to take advantage of this wonderful opportunity to get an education and meet a lot of great people, or do you want to come home and look up the rear-end of a mule the rest of your life? You've got a decision to make. But whatever you decide, please quit calling your mother and worrying her to death!" That conversation hit me like a slap in the face. I realized I couldn't call my mother anymore because she was spilling the beans. So I made the best decision and stayed at Auburn.

As a member of Auburn's 1963 freshman team, Bryan played quarterback for Dooley, and the two developed a close relationship. However, as Bryan prepared to move to the varsity squad, Dooley was hired by the University of Georgia.

"It was tough," Bryan said. "We had become close and I hated seeing Coach Dooley leave. I will say this though, having Coach Dooley at a rival school definitely made the Auburn-Georgia game more important."

In the end, Dooley's decision to chase Bryan down in 1963 proved costly for UGA. As a sophomore in 1964, Bryan played quarterback against Dooley's Dogs and helped lead Auburn to a 14–7 victory. Bryan rushed for 89 yards and a touchdown, while Heisman Trophy finalist Tucker Frederickson added 101 yards and the other score. It was Bryan's first game starting at quarterback.

Tom Bryan (19) sprints for a touchdown as Georgia cheerleaders watch in disbelief. *Auburn University Library Special Collections.*

A year later, after splitting time at quarterback with Alex Bowden, Auburn coach Ralph "Shug" Jordan decided to move Bryan to fullback late in the 1965 season. Unfortunately for Dooley, Bryan's coming-out party was again against UGA. Although Jenkins's fumble is what most of Athens remembers, Bryan picked apart Georgia's defense, averaging eight and a half yards per carry, highlighted by a forty-one-yard touchdown run in the first quarter. After Auburn's dramatic 21–19 victory, the *Birmingham News* printed a conversation between Dooley and his former player.

"You're the best fullback in the league, Tom, but why did you have to pick today to show it?" Dooley asked Bryan inside Sanford Stadium. "You've really made a great adjustment to fullback. I've never seen anybody make a better one."

Furman Bisher raved about Bryan's efforts in the *Atlanta Journal-Constitution*:

> *Georgia was able to match Auburn in every way but one—Tom Bryan, a reformed quarterback now belonging to the fullback union. This was Bryan's day. The 195-pound junior from Hartford, Ala., ran like a barefoot boy on an asphalt street at high noon in August. He gained 29 more yards on the ground than the whole Georgia team. He scored the first touchdown and set up the third. When nothing else would work against Georgia's erratic defense, Bryan did.*

After going 2-0 against UGA in 1964 and 1965, Bryan suffered injuries his senior season and was unable to play against Georgia in 1966. With Bryan sidelined, Dooley beat Auburn for the first time en route to UGA becoming SEC co-champions.

"It was a special situation between Coach Dooley and myself," said Bryan, now a State Farm Insurance agent in Opelika, Alabama. "He's always held a special place in my heart for reaching out and saving me as a freshman. He made it possible for me to get an education and play SEC football. Without Vince Dooley, who knows where I'd be?"

16

DOOLEY'S FIRST—1966

GEORGIA 21, AUBURN 13

Kirby Moore's most vivid memory of beating Auburn in 1966 isn't overcoming a 13–0 halftime deficit. Nor is it playing on a field soaked in mud or clinching a share of the SEC championship. Oddly enough, what Georgia's quarterback remembers most is lying in a hotel bathtub the night before kickoff.

"I felt horrible at our team hotel," Moore said. "Absolutely horrible. Trainers kept soaking me in a tub, trying to lower my fever."

In the end, Moore played and performed well. Despite being shutout in the first half, Georgia stormed back, scoring twenty-one unanswered points to stun forty-seven thousand fans at Cliff Hare Stadium. Interestingly for Moore, the outcome may not have been possible without an all-night drive by four friends from Waynesboro, Georgia.

As a native of Dothan, Alabama, Kirby Moore told Auburn and Alabama football recruiters he planned to focus collegiately on baseball—which he had every intention of doing. Fortunately for Georgia, its head baseball coach, "Big Jim" Whatley, was also a football recruiter for the state of Alabama. With Whatley leading the charge, Moore was told he could play both football and baseball in Athens, prompting the two-sport athlete to commit to UGA.

"When it came out I was playing both, [Alabama] Coach Bear Bryant called and goes, 'Hey, we thought you were playing baseball,'" Moore remembered. "I said, 'Well, I changed my mind.'"

Bryant offered Moore a scholarship, but the Alabama teenager honored his pledge to Whatley. After redshirting in 1963, Vince Dooley was hired at Georgia in 1964, which led to Moore quickly ending his plans to swing a bat. "If I had told Coach Dooley I wanted to play baseball, that would've been the same as saying I wanted to move to North Vietnam," Moore said. "If you played football, you focused on football."

So that's what Moore did. For three summers, however, Moore didn't return to work in Dothan. Instead, he got a job in Waynesboro, Georgia, about twenty miles south of Augusta, working as a cotton scout. As part of the insecticide business, Moore would meet each summer with local farmers who used his product in cotton gins. Moore lived with a local family. He was loaned a Jeep to make rounds. To put it mildly, Waynesboro became his home away from home.

"Those folks in Waynesboro treated me so well," Moore said. "I got to be very close with a lot of people there." So close that while fighting his pregame illness, Moore received a call in his hotel room. On the other line were four friends from Waynesboro who suddenly decided they wanted to come to Auburn.

"It's 10 at night and I'm dealing with the flu," Moore said. "Well, they called and asked if I could get them in. I said, 'This is the biggest game in the world. If we beat Auburn, we win the SEC.' They said, 'Well, we're coming.'"

In the dead of night, four boys left Waynesboro and drove toward Auburn in search of Georgia's team hotel. When Moore awoke Saturday morning, his friends were waiting in the parking lot. Still without tickets, Moore told his buddies they could sleep in his hotel room while he took part in meetings and a pregame meal.

"Coach Dooley would've killed me if he knew what was going on," Moore said. "Luckily, before our team meeting I was able to find four sideline passes."

KIRBY MOORE AND THE REST OF GEORGIA'S TEAM started slow. Playing in sloppy conditions, Auburn quarterback Loran Carter, of Dalton, Georgia, scored on a thirty-six-yard run in the first quarter. Later in the period, Carter threw a thirty-two-yard touchdown pass to receiver Freddie Hyatt. Suddenly, the Tigers were in front 13–0 and Moore's physical condition didn't seem promising. Moments before halftime, Moore ran a quarterback sweep, fell out of bounds and couldn't rise on his own. In a state of exhaustion, the quarterback looked up from the muddy sideline and saw four familiar faces from Waynesboro.

"They picked me up and said, 'Go back in there!'" Moore remembered.

The play provided an adrenaline rush for Moore, as did halftime pep talks from teammates and Dooley. According to UGA wide receiver Hardy King, who sat next to Moore in the locker room, Dooley made one point to his players. "We're trailing 13–0, and Kirby is sick as he can be," King recalled.

> *But after all the players spoke, Coach Dooley was the last one to say something. Dooley looked at us and goes, "If we play exactly how we did in the first half, we'll win this football game." You know, I was shocked he said that because we're losing, but I thought to myself, "OK, let's do this."*

Coming out of halftime, Georgia seized control, scoring fourteen points in the third quarter to take a one-point lead. The go-ahead score came with thirty-one seconds left in the period, when Moore found King crossing over the middle for a fifty-two-yard touchdown. It was King's only touchdown in 1966, but the play proved instrumental in helping Dooley defeat his mentor, Ralph "Shug" Jordan, for the first time.

"Kirby hit me right between the three and the three," said King, who wore No. 33. "That pass was a bullet and I never looked back to see if anyone was chasing me."

As King approached the goal line, he dove near the right corner.

"That dang mud was so bad I just about slid out of the end zone," King remembered. "I'll tell you what, that was the biggest play of my career. I still have the jersey framed in my home, along with articles from that day in Auburn. I'll never forget that moment as long as I live."

UGA fullback Ronnie Jenkins added an insurance score in the fourth quarter, while Georgia's defense shutout Auburn over the final three periods. After the game, an estimated ten thousand fans waited for the Bulldogs to arrive at Athens Municipal Airport. When the SEC co-champions landed at 7:15 p.m., fans chanted, "Dooley for governor!" and "We're No. 1!" The crowd was so eager to congratulate the team that fans rushed the planes before propellers were shut off. As for Moore, the quarterback was nowhere to be found. With the Bulldogs having a week off before facing Georgia Tech, Dooley didn't force players to return home with the team. Being from Alabama, Moore stayed the night in Auburn with three Dothan High School teammates who had become Auburn students.

"We all went out and had the best night," said Moore, who practices law in Macon, Georgia. "I even ran into a few Auburn players, but we just shook hands and said, 'Good game.'"

Still, it's getting lifted up by his Waynesboro crew that Moore hasn't forgotten fifty years later.

"Back in Waynesboro, those four guys told everybody, 'Kirby fell out-of-bounds and we all thought he was dead,'" Moore said, laughing. "It's the truth, though—if they weren't on the sideline, I don't think I would've gotten up."

17

UGA II POSES FOR PICTURES—1968

GEORGIA 17, AUBURN 3

Every August, fans line the sidewalk outside Sanford Stadium with hopes of getting a ticket to meet Uga, Georgia's iconic mascot. But the fascination of being photographed with the bulldog hasn't always been this way. In fact, following Georgia's 1968 victory at Auburn, it was Sonny Seiler, Uga's owner, making the photo requests.

"This was before Uga had become really popular," said Mike Cavan, Georgia's quarterback in 1968. "Well, after we won the SEC in Auburn, Sonny came to me in the locker room and asked if I'd take a picture with the dog."

Cavan joyfully agreed and still has it framed in his Athens home. As for Seiler, he also has a copy displayed in his Savannah residence.

"It's the exact opposite these days," Cavan said. "Now, people are asking to *get their* picture with the dog."

Added Seiler: "I'll tell you something, that's one of my favorite photographs ever. We had the best time celebrating after beating Auburn that day. I loved that 1968 team—I love Mike Cavan."

Uga II never rose to national fame, but Georgia's 1968 victory at Cliff Hare Stadium centered the Southeastern Conference spotlight on Athens. The victory earned Vince Dooley his second SEC title in three years, while marking the second time since 1959 that Georgia prevented Auburn from taking the crown.

All About Erk's Defense

Nine years after 1959, it was again winner-take-all for Auburn and Georgia. Despite losing its season opener to Southern Methodist and later falling to Georgia Tech, Auburn was 4-0 against conference foes and was coming off a 28–14 upset of No. 5 Tennessee. Similar to Auburn, UGA was also unbeaten in the SEC (4-0-1) and riding high after a 51–0 destruction of Florida a week before in Jacksonville. Georgia's lone blemishes were a 17–17 tie to Tennessee and a non-conference tie against Houston.

"At the beginning of the year, we set a goal to become SEC champions," said Bill Stanfill, UGA's All-American lineman. "We had every plan of accomplishing that mission."

UGA fullback Brad Johnson (41) plows over Auburn defenders in 1968. *Auburn University Library Special Collections.*

No. 5 Georgia entered the contest as three-point favorites, but pregame predictions didn't matter to the home crowd. In all, 50,009 spectators flooded Cliff Hare Stadium—the largest at the time in Auburn history. Also on hand were representatives from the Orange Bowl, Sugar Bowl, Cotton Bowl, Sun Bowl, Gator Bowl and Peach Bowl. In the end, UGA got the Sugar Bowl, Auburn the Sun Bowl. And it was largely because of Erk Russell's defensive strategy. "We had the bald-headed genius," Stanfill said. "I've played a lot of football in my lifetime but no defensive coach was better than Erk Russell."

With a modest ground attack, Auburn relied heavily on quarterback Loran Carter's arm and speedy receiver Tim Christian. In its three games before facing UGA, Carter had combined to toss nine touchdowns in victories over Miami, Florida and Tennessee. None of those secondaries, however, were led by All-American Jake Scott. Daring Auburn to throw deep, Scott picked off two passes in the opening half, leading Tigers coach Ralph "Shug" Jordan to alter his game plan. Eventually, Jordan removed his star quarterback in the fourth period in favor of backup Tommy Traylor. For the game, Auburn had twenty-three yards rushing and sixty-three passing.

"I don't think Auburn would've scored if we stayed out there another two days," Cavan said. "Our defense was that determined."

Opening the game, Auburn struck first, as John Riley converted a twenty-eight-yard field goal in the first quarter. Georgia matched the score with a Jim McCullough kick in the second period. Then, on the ensuing kickoff, arguably the biggest play of the contest occurred. Upon receiving the kick, Auburn's Mike Currier eluded Scott and seemed destined to return the kickoff for a touchdown. But as Cliff Hare Stadium erupted, little-known sophomore Ken Shaw tackled Currier from behind at Georgia's eighteen-yard line.

"I was the end man on the opposite side of the field," Shaw remembered. "I can still see [Currier] break loose and I remember thinking, 'I have got to get an angle on him.'"

Oddly enough, Dooley had hoped to redshirt Shaw in 1968, going as far as sitting the sophomore for the first two games of the season. However, due to injuries, Dooley activated the backup receiver before playing South Carolina, and the Atlanta native started on special teams the remainder of the year. His biggest contribution undoubtedly occurred

Vince Dooley gives advice to quarterback Mike Cavan during Georgia's 17–3 victory over Auburn in 1968. *Auburn University Library Special Collections.*

on November 16. "I had two things running through my head," Shaw recalled. "First, I have to get there. And second, I absolutely cannot miss this tackle. When I got back to the sideline, defensive backs coach Billy Kinard ran up and gave me a huge hug. Coach Kinard said, 'You may have just won this ball game.'"

Following Shaw's tackle, UGA's defense held tight, and this time, Riley missed from twenty-five yards to keep the score at 3–3. With all the momentum now to the visitors, Cavan connected with receiver Kent Lawrence for a twenty-two-yard score, giving Georgia its first lead of the game. Later in the second period, Cavan found the end zone on a one-yard sneak to pull ahead, 17–3.

"Getting ahead by two touchdowns was more than enough for our defense," Cavan said. "We decided to play very conservative in the second half, and I think Coach Dooley did that out of respect for Coach Jordan. Look, I'm not saying we would have scored more touchdowns—Auburn had a good defense. It just seemed clear to me that Coach Dooley had no intention of running up the score."

The ultimate sign of respect for Russell's defense came after halftime. With each of Georgia's seventeen first-half points coming off Auburn turnovers, Jordan elected to kick off to UGA to start the third quarter instead of taking the ball. The strategy was somewhat successful, as UGA didn't score, but Auburn couldn't find an offensive rhythm either. Following the game, Zipp Newman, sports editor emeritus of the *Birmingham News*, wrote, "I have seen a lot of great Georgia teams. This could be the best, providing it shows in a bowl what it showed here Saturday afternoon when pupil Vince Dooley was at his best against his old professor, Shug Jordan."

As the clock ran out, Cavan rushed toward his head coach in an effort to present Dooley with the game ball. However, as excitement overflowed, Cavan accidentally took Dooley to the ground while handing over the keepsake. Speaking to media members after the game, Dooley suggested, "I bet that's the only tackle Mike ever made in his life."

"We all got knocked down when the clock ran out," Cavan remembered. "That game, becoming conference champions, that was the culmination of our entire year."

After starting unranked in September, the 1968 Bulldogs finished the regular season 8-0-2, earning an invitation to the Sugar Bowl. Georgia lost in New Orleans, 16–2, to Arkansas. Looking back on the year, Cavan is quick to mention team chemistry.

UGA's Mark Stewart breaks up a pass intended for Tim Christian (85). *Auburn University Library Special Collections.*

"We had unbelievable senior leadership," Cavan said. "Now, we had some characters on that team, too. You talk about Bill Stanfill, Jake Scott—I mean gee manetti. Brad Johnson, Dennis Hughes. We had some characters, but every one of those characters had character."

BILL STANFILL

In 1968, Georgia's defense allowed 9.8 points per contest, which ranked No. 1 nationally. A large reason for its success was due to Stanfill's constant pressure on opposing quarterbacks. But Stanfill, of Cairo, Georgia, nearly played collegiately at Auburn. The future consensus All-American verbally committed to Tigers defensive coordinator Hal Herring before family members began pressuring the prized recruit.

"I had some family pressure telling me to stay in state, and I listened," said Stanfill, who passed away the week of the 2016 Auburn-Georgia game. "In the end, it was the best decision I ever made. I won two SEC championships [1966 and 1968] and was able to learn from Coach Russell."

Stanfill switched his commitment in the final month, but it wasn't due to a lack of effort from Herring. "Vince Dooley and Hal Herring were both at my house when I was deciding who to sign with," Stanfill said. "When I picked Georgia, Coach Herring got up and left."

SUGAR BOWL CONTROVERSY

Seven days before the Deep South's Oldest Rivalry, Georgia unleashed a 51–0 beat-down on Florida, climbing from No. 9 to No. 5 in national polls. Seemingly overnight, UGA became one of the most desired bowl teams in the country, and Sugar Bowl officials immediately made their voice heard. In the week leading up to Auburn, the Sugar Bowl offered UGA athletic director Joel Eaves a guaranteed spot in New Orleans, under one condition: UGA had to commit before November 16 because Sugar Bowl officials feared Georgia would select the highly regarded Orange Bowl if they beat Auburn.

In a column by *Atlanta Journal-Constitution* sports editor Jesse Outlar, the journalist wrote:

> *In brief, a New Orleans source outlines the bizarre script. The Sugar Bowl, unexcited about Georgia until the 51–0 Florida romp, belatedly decided the Bulldogs were the best bowl team in the SEC. The Orange Bowl put the same rating on the Bulldogs, but the Orange Bowl, a very confident group, wanted to await the outcome at Auburn. While figuring they had nothing to lose, they apparently lost Georgia.*

To the displeasure of some players, including Jake Scott, Georgia accepted the early offer from New Orleans before traveling to the Plains. Largely due to the decision, Scott had a falling-out with Dooley following the 1968 season and elected to leave Athens early. In two seasons at UGA, Scott led the SEC in interceptions in 1967 and 1968. The safety had ten interceptions, including two against Auburn, in 1968 and was named SEC Player of the Year. For all his on-field heroics, however, Scott may be best remembered in Athens for riding a motorcycle across the roof of Stegeman Coliseum.

18

GEORGIA'S REVENGE—1980

GEORGIA 31, AUBURN 21

The game was far from an instant classic. Georgia led 31–7 in the third quarter, while Auburn never pulled to within single digits in the second half. However, Georgia's victory at Jordan-Hare Stadium not only clinched the 1980 conference title, it also eased the pain of 1978 and 1979. A sign in Georgia's visiting dressing room read, "Payback two years—no sugar."

In '78 and '79, Georgia would have been SEC champions and earned a trip to New Orleans with a victory in the Deep South's Oldest Rivalry. Instead, Auburn twice played spoiler, tying the Bulldogs in 1978 before routing Georgia, 33–13, in 1979.

Following those two seasons, Georgia was aware of the dangers Auburn presented. But to ensure his team's focus, Vince Dooley asked UGA legend Frank Sinkwich to speak to his players after Thursday's practice. Why Sinkwich? It's simple: Prior to November 15, 1980, the last time Georgia had been ranked No. 1 was on November 21, 1942, and that UGA team was upset by a 4-4-1 Auburn squad. Thirty-eight years later, Dooley wanted to ensure a similar outcome wasn't in the making.

"There was only one way we were leaving Auburn," remembered UGA defensive back Scott Woerner, who smoked a cigar following the win. "That was with a victory. I promise you we weren't leaving town any other way."

Thousands of UGA supporters migrated to Auburn to witness the contest, while Stegeman Coliseum held a viewing party for those who stayed in Athens. As for the game itself, a bizarre chain of events proved to be Auburn's undoing. Leading the No. 1 Bulldogs 7–3 in the second

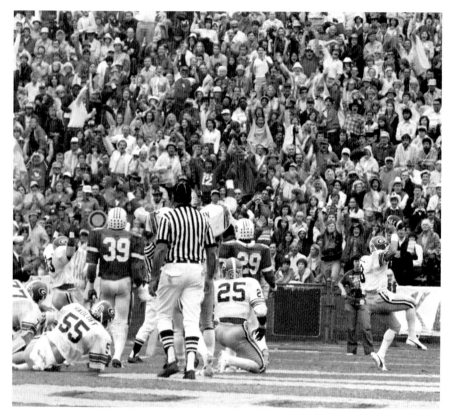

Buck Belue celebrates after scoring a touchdown at Jordan-Hare Stadium. *Morris Communications.*

quarter, Auburn (who entered the game 0-4 in the SEC) allowed twenty-one points in a nine-minute span to end its upset bid. The first somewhat odd play came when freshman Freddie Gilbert returned a blocked punt for a touchdown in the second period: 10–7 Georgia. The next happened nine seconds before halftime, when UGA quarterback Buck Belue fumbled on Auburn's one-yard line. Without a timeout, the half seemed over, but officials paused play with five seconds left to determine possession. When Georgia was deemed to have recovered, the Bulldogs quickly regrouped, and Belue called "clock play," a design UGA had practiced for this exact situation. After receiving the snap, Belue lobbed a wobbly touchdown to Norris Brown as time expired: 17–7.

Adding to Auburn's displeasure, Tigers defensive coordinator Paul Davis had stepped in the end zone to dispute the fumble ruling. Auburn was assessed a fifteen-yard penalty on the third-quarter kickoff, which ignited trickery from Dooley. Now kicking from Auburn's forty-five, UGA recovered an onside kick and drove for another score: 24–7.

"I asked [Paul Davis] what in the world he was doing," Auburn head coach Doug Barfield recalled. "He said, 'I got carried away and thought time had ran out.' That fourteen-point swing at halftime hurt so bad. We needed every break to go our way and it simply didn't happen."

Auburn rallied for two late scores, but the outcome was hardly in doubt. Just like that, the Bulldogs had avenged 1978 and 1979.

"Auburn was the difference between our senior class leaving with three SEC championships and a national championship, and possibly being the greatest class ever," said Frank Ros, captain of the 1980 team. "Instead, we left with one SEC title and one national championship."

Ros married the former Jan Floyd, Miss Auburn 1981, whom he didn't know at the time of his final SEC game. Both were seniors during the 1980 season and Ros says, "It's given me bragging rights for life."

Auburn—which fired Barfield after the season—finished 0-6 in the SEC, while the Bulldogs went 6-0. For Georgia's senior class, it was their lone victory over Auburn, and their fans weren't afraid to celebrate. As the game ended, more than a handful of UGA supporters sprinted onto the Jordan-Hare Stadium field, prompting a brief fight between fan bases under one goalpost. As the scuffle continued, Auburn's public address announcer begged over the loudspeakers: "We can appreciate your enthusiasm for your victory, but please leave the field. Do not celebrate around the goalposts!"

After finishing its regular season unbeaten, the Bulldogs captured their only Associated Press national title with a 17–10 triumph over Notre Dame.

"That win at Auburn was so huge for us," said UGA kicker Rex Robinson, a senior in 1980. "Auburn had become the thorn in our side after those games in 1978 and '79. We went 1-2-1 against them during my four years, but that one victory was really, really sweet."

LIMITING HERSCHEL

Going into the game, Auburn's strategy was no secret: stop Herschel Walker. For the most part, the Tigers did exactly that, holding the freshman sensation to seventy-seven yards on twenty-seven attempts. But Belue (who entered the contest with minus twenty-six rushing yards on seventy-six attempts) and reserve tailback Carnie Norris made up the difference. To the surprise of

Auburn, Belue matched Walker with seventy-seven yards on the ground, while Norris gained seventy-two yards on ten fourth-quarter carries. The morning after the game, an article by the *Montgomery Advertiser* sports editor Phillip Marshall stated, "It was billed as a battle of the tailbacks, but Georgia quarterback Buck Belue stole the show."

Auburn tailback James Brooks outshone Walker with eighty-five yards on twenty-one attempts and left Jordan-Hare Stadium unimpressed with the No. 1 team in the nation. "They didn't look like no No. 1 team to me," Brooks told media outlets after the game. "If they're No. 1, we're No. 2." Also underwhelmed was Auburn quarterback Charles Thomas. In the locker room after the loss, Thomas told reporters, "The best team lost today. They got all the good breaks and we got all the bad ones."

All that mattered, however, was the final score. As UGA arrived home, thousands of students swarmed its team buses as the clock neared 10:00 p.m. According to an *Atlanta Journal* article by Susan Wells, "As each of their heroes walked down a path through the screaming fans, his name was chanted. When Wrightsville freshman tailback Herschel Walker got off the bus, pandemonium broke out. The crowd surged forward and cheered him for several minutes as he stood grinning at them."

THE MOMENTUM SHIFT

For the only time in his career, Greg Bell was a captain on November 15, 1980. He was also responsible for the play that shifted momentum. With both parents and grandparents in attendance, Bell, from East Lake, Alabama, blew past Auburn's line and blocked a punt in the second quarter. At the time, UGA trailed 7–3 until teammate Freddie Gilbert scooped up the block and returned it twenty-seven yards for the go-ahead touchdown.

Plainly put, the circumstances behind Bell's achievement were as unlikely as him being presented with the game ball after the win. Bell, a senior in 1980, had never attempted to block a punt during his first forty-three games in red and black. However, the week before playing Florida, UGA defensive end Dale Carver got hurt and was removed from special teams. When defensive coordinator Erk Russell asked for a volunteer replacement, Bell jumped at the opportunity to play right end. "I had been in the film room for four years and had some ideas about how to get to the punter," Bell said.

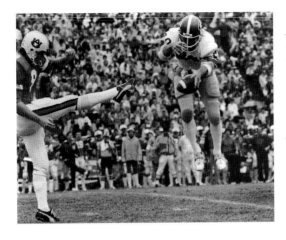

Greg Bell blocks a punt at Jordan-Hare Stadium on November 15, 1980. *UGA Athletic Department.*

Bell's unique strategy almost worked in Jacksonville. A week later, it was successful at Auburn. Against Florida and Auburn, on the first punt attempt of the game, Bell lined up on the outside of the last lineman and did a swoop around the blocker. On the second punt, Bell positioned himself nose-to-nose with the lineman and rushed around right end. Finally, on the third attempt, Bell lined up slightly inside of the lineman, took a jab step to the outside, then darted inward.

"When I did that jab step, both the Florida and Auburn blocker pulled his foot to the outside," Bell said. "That left me free to run inside untouched."

Against Florida, an up-back halted Bell's momentum before he reached the punter. Against Auburn, however, the up-back was focused on Will Forts—Georgia's other end—and didn't notice Bell. "I basically had a twelve-yard sprint to the ball," said Bell, who was named SEC Special Teams Player of the Week.

Bell almost outran the kick.

"I got in the backfield so fast that I had to jump straight up because I was about to overrun the ball," he said. "We had really come out flat against Auburn, like we did all four of my years at Georgia, but that block got our juices going. From that point on, it really changed the momentum and before you knew it the score was 31–7."

In the years after graduating from UGA, Bell would occasionally be invited back to Auburn by Mike Hubbard, who earned his degree from Georgia before being hired by Auburn's sports information department in the 1980s. The two would sit in the press box together and would often be called out by one of Auburn's most famous faces.

"I'd walk into the press box and each time David Housel [Auburn's former athletic director] would say, 'Oh, no! Not you,'" said Bell, laughing. "Housel would tell everybody, 'You see that spot on the field? That's where he did that horrible thing to us.'"

INSIDE THE RIVALRY

Jimmy Womack never played in the National Football League. He didn't strive for personal fame or crave self-promotion. That simply wasn't Womack.

On May 10, 2015, Womack, the starting fullback on Georgia's 1980 team, died following complications from hip surgery, ending a life of trials and triumph. The hardships were centered on drug addiction. His on-field conquests revolved around two great tailbacks: James Brooks (Warner Robins High School) and Herschel Walker (UGA).

Growing up in Warner Robins, Brooks and Womack connected at a young age, as they first teamed together as seven-year-olds in youth football. They played middle school football on the same squad and then partnered to help Warner Robins High win the 1976 state championship and finish the year ranked No. 1 in the country.

"Jimmy mentioned one time about playing together in college," Brooks said, "but I wanted him to have the spotlight for himself. I wanted Jimmy to step out of my shadow and show people what he could do. I'm the one that said, 'I think you should go establish yourself at Georgia.' At one point, I even went to [Warner Robins head coach Robert Davis] and asked Coach Davis if Jimmy could take my spot on the high school All Star team."

In the end, Brooks—despite immense pressure from hometown friends to attend UGA—chose Auburn. Womack signed with Georgia.

"Coach Davis was a Bulldogs fan," Brooks recalled.

> He would hint that I should play at Georgia, but there were two reasons why I didn't: First, I wanted to be different. I've always wanted to be different. And second, William Andrews was a senior in high school when I was entering tenth grade and we met one day. I told him, "I hear you're going to Auburn," and we kept talking. He finally said, "Man, it would be great if you come, too." Auburn had a lot of talent with William Andrews and Joe Cribbs, but that didn't matter to me. I loved competition. In fact, when I got to Auburn in 1977, I told Cribbs, "Joe, you might be the starter right now but that won't be for long."

At Auburn, Brooks set records in rushing yards (3,253), kick-return yards (1,726) and all-purpose yards (5,596), while garnering All-American honors. Womack rushed for 803 yards and two touchdowns during his career at Georgia, including a high of 395 yards in 1978. Similar to high school, however, Womack became best known for paving the way for a star running back. This time, it was Walker.

Arguably the most memorable play of Womack's career was springing Walker loose for the go-ahead touchdown in the Sugar Bowl win over Notre Dame. And while media outlets gushed over Brooks and Walker, both iconic backs knew Womack deserved attention. In 2014, Brooks was inducted into the Georgia Sports Hall of Fame at a ceremony in Macon, a twenty-minute drive on Interstate 75 from Womack's home in Warner Robins.

"I wanted so bad for Jimmy to be there—I even reserved him a ticket," Brooks said. "In my speech, I was going to tell him how grateful I was for everything he did for me. I was going to make it clear how special he was. I had it all planned out."

With failing health, Womack was hospitalized the week of the ceremony and couldn't attend. Less than a year later, he passed away at fifty-six.

19

SUGAR FALLS FROM JORDAN-HARE—1982

GEORGIA 19, AUBURN 14

The Sugar Bowl, the championship, swinging and I mean swinging on a little thread here. Every single play means something now or you're gone. Total war in Auburn. Complete, total war!
—*Larry Munson, UGA radio announcer*

John Lastinger had been warned all week.

The Saturday before facing Auburn, Georgia's junior quarterback had taken his team to Jacksonville and unleashed a 44–0 beat-down on Florida. The win lifted the unbeaten Bulldogs from No. 3 to No. 1 in national polls and placed an even larger bull's-eye (if that was possible) on UGA's back. All the while, Lastinger assumed he'd be welcomed to the Loveliest Village on the Plains by a hostile Auburn crowd.

"It was a cool, beautiful day for football," Lastinger recalled. "But the biggest thing I remember was how remarkably quiet it was at Jordan-Hare Stadium. It really was. Everyone talked about it being such a tough place to play but I just thought to myself, 'Well, it doesn't seem that tough to me.'"

The crowd remained tame for three quarters, until a running back nicknamed "Little Train" awoke the seventy-four-thousand-person sleeping giant. More than anything, though, the 1982 playing of the Deep South's Oldest Rivalry was a battle between champion and challenger.

UGA quarterback John Lastinger attempts a pass against Auburn in 1982. *The Augusta Chronicle.*

Auburn freshman Bo Jackson gets tackled by UGA defenders Stan Dooley and Terry Hoage. *Morris Communications.*

The champion was UGA, which had won consecutive Southeastern Conference titles in 1980 and 1981. Georgia had made back-to-back Sugar Bowl appearances, including winning a national title in 1980. It was Herschel Walker's final season in Athens, a year he rushed for 1,752 yards, sixteen touchdowns and captured the Heisman Trophy. On top of everything, UGA hadn't lost an SEC game since Auburn upset the Bulldogs in 1979.

The challenger was Auburn. It was Pat Dye's second season, and his team was inching closer to overtaking Georgia on the mountaintop. After going winless in the SEC in 1980, Auburn was in line to earn its first conference championship since 1957 with wins over Georgia and Alabama. It had a talented freshman named Bo Jackson; a shifty junior in Lionel James; and a hard-nosed defense that resembled the group with rings in Athens.

The Wednesday before kickoff, *Athens Banner-Herald* sports editor Blake Giles wrote a column warning UGA fans of what stood ahead of them: "If you thought defending the Mississippi State wishbone was tough, wait until you get a look at the Auburn wishbone. Stopping halfback Lionel James is like trying to catch a butterfly with a bottle cap. Stopping Ron O'Neal is like trying to derail a train with a toothpick. Stopping Bo Jackson is like trying to abort a missile launching with a tennis racket. Stopping Randy Campbell is like trying to break the access code for the computer at the Chase Manhattan Bank with a hand-held calculator."

In the end, the champion prevailed in what Vince Dooley called "the hardest game he could ever remember."

GREETING THE BULLDOGS AS THEY ARRIVED in Auburn was a sign that hung off the side of Jordan-Hare Stadium. Its message: "Herschel Eats Quiche," a reference to Bruce Feirstein's 1982 book *Real Men Don't Eat Quiche*. On the door of Auburn's locker room were more words of encouragement, including a sticker that said, "Kill Herschel."

Unfortunately for the Tigers, no combination of letters slowed down No. 34 on November 13, 1982. Vying for his third conference title since arriving in Athens, Walker put Georgia ahead 10–7 with a forty-seven-yard burst in the second quarter—his longest score through ten games in 1982. But the Bulldog lead didn't last. On the third play of the fourth period, Auburn quarterback Randy Campbell pitched to Lionel "Little Train" James, whose five-foot, seven-inch frame found a hole. He shifted. He sprinted. He eluded. Eighty-seven yards later, Auburn was stunningly ahead, 14–13.

Tigers quarterback Randy Campbell (14) is brought down. *The* Augusta Chronicle.

"As quiet as Jordan-Hare had been all game, it was equally as deafening when Lionel James busted loose," Lastinger said. "I'm telling you, that place went crazy."

James's burst put Auburn in front, but it also placed Georgia in familiar territory. Despite being undefeated, UGA had come from behind in six of its first nine games, starting on Labor Day with a victory over defending national champion Clemson. Quite simply, Georgia was used to playing from behind. It was also used to pulling ahead. That script didn't change on November 13. After taking over on its twenty-yard line, Georgia ran thirteen plays—converting four third downs—before Walker found the goal line. The drive was sustained on four crucial plays. On third and five at Auburn's forty-nine, Walker plowed over left tackle for 6 yards. On third and six from Auburn's thirty-nine, Lastinger, who completed only four of nine passes for 43 yards, found freshman Herman Archie for 17 yards. On third and one from the thirteen, Walker lunged for 2. Finally, on third and goal from the three, Walker slid between offensive linemen Warren Gray and Guy McIntyre for the touchdown: 19–14 UGA. The Heisman Trophy winner totaled 38 of his 177 yards on the crucial drive.

After Walker scored, Auburn was left with 8:42 to answer. Instead, what happened will forever be remembered as arguably Larry Munson's

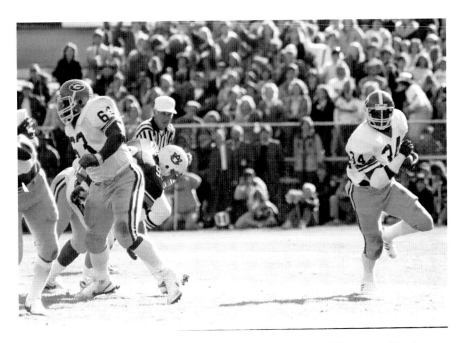

Herschel Walker, the 1982 Heisman Trophy winner, finished with 177 yards rushing in Georgia's 19–14 win at Jordan-Hare Stadium. *The* Augusta Chronicle.

greatest radio call. Behind the legs of Campbell, James and Jackson, Auburn marched to Georgia's fourteen-yard line as the clock neared 2:00. Through the airwaves, Munson pleaded with his Bulldogs, continuously telling the champions to "Hunker Down!" The Bulldogs rose to the occasion, helped by a procedure penalty which made it first and fifteen from the nineteen-yard line.

On first down, Bo Jackson was stopped for a two-yard loss.

"Ball back on the twenty-one and it's second down now and seventeen," Munson blared. "With 2:05 to go, Auburn trying to break our hearts here! 19 to 14 and the Dogs lead. Again you guys, Hunker Down!"

On second down, UGA defensive end Dale Carver sacked Campbell for a nine-yard loss.

"Carver got him from behind back on the 30!" Munson exclaimed. "Carver blitzed from the right-end corner. Carver blew in unprotected.... Oh man, two big plays—eighty-four seconds....I hate to keep saying it but Hunker Down! If you didn't hear me, you guys, Hunker Down!"

On third down, Campbell completed a pass to tight end Ed West, who stumbled at Georgia's twenty-one as the clock ticked below sixty seconds.

"Fourth and 17," Munson stated. "I know I'm asking a lot, you guys, but *hunker it down one more time!*"

On fourth down, Campbell's desperation heave toward Mike Edwards was broken up in the end zone by defensive backs Jeff Sanchez and Ronnie Harris. As Sanchez leapt for joy, UGA had clinched Vince Dooley's sixth and final SEC title.

"The Dogs broke it up!" Munson exclaimed. "They broke it up! They broke it up! Ronnie Harris and Jeff Sanchez got up in the air—we had pressure up the middle. ...I won't ask you to do that again, you guys."

Following a pair of kneel downs from Lastinger, the clock ticked toward 0:00. "23, 22, 21—clock running, *running!*" Munson proudly screamed. "Oh, look at the sugar falling out of the sky! Look at the sugar falling out of the sky!"

Georgia completed an undefeated regular season with a victory over Georgia Tech, but the Bulldogs were upset, 27–23, by Penn State in the Sugar Bowl.

20

AUBURN'S REVENGE—1987

AUBURN 27, GEORGIA 11

Jeff Burger hurried toward the fifty-yard line as time expired at Sanford Stadium. Normally, midfield is reserved for opposing coaches to shake hands, but on November. 14, 1987, Auburn's senior quarterback made sure he was there to greet Vince Dooley.

"The first thing out of my mouth was, 'Coach, never been scared of competition. Good game,'" Burger recalled.

A confused Pat Dye, who was standing behind his quarterback, shook hands with Dooley, then glared at Burger. "What the hell was that about?" Dye asked.

GROWING UP IN CEDARTOWN, GEORGIA, Burger's childhood dream was to play for Dooley in Athens. But unlike most Peach State kids, Burger's dream was almost a reality. As a junior and senior, Burger led Cedartown High School to a combined 22-2 record and earned a scholarship offer from UGA. However, with additional offers from Auburn, Alabama and Clemson, Burger didn't immediately commit to Dooley. He wanted to weigh his options—including the possibility of playing collegiate baseball.

"A lot of smaller schools wanted me to come play football and baseball," Burger said. "I just didn't want to rush into a decision."

In December 1982, Burger and Cedartown head coach John Hill made the trek to Athens for a recruiting visit. The heralded passer watched as Georgia prepared for the national championship game against Penn State. He got to meet tailback Herschel Walker. He even sat in on a quarterback

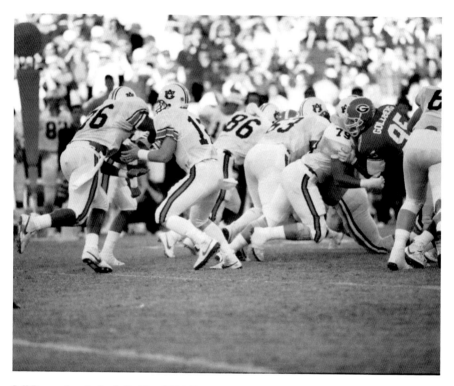

Jeff Burger hands the ball off as UGA lineman Bill Goldberg (95) comes through the line. *Morris Communications.*

meeting with offensive coordinator George Haffner. "I was in dreamland," Burger admitted.

Those emotions, however, quickly changed. As practice began, Burger noticed eleven quarterbacks dressed out, five in one practice area and six in another. With depth clearly scattered on each field, Burger began to wonder how many quarterbacks Georgia planned to sign in its 1983 class.

"Every college kind of told you what they were doing—how many QBs they were going to sign," Burger said. "Teams were upfront about where they stood in recruiting."

About midway through Georgia's practice, Dooley approached Burger to check on the recruit. A star struck teenager made small talk with the coach before gathering the nerve to ask how many signal callers he planned to bring in.

"Coach Dooley looked at me and said, 'Son, if you're scared of competition then Georgia might not be the place for you,'" Burger remembered.

When Coach Dooley said that, it embarrassed me. I just thought, "My gosh, he thinks I'm scared of competition." Now put yourself in my shoes; this is Vince Dooley. A legend. I'm just a teenager wanting to know the situation, especially after seeing 11 guys warm up.

Following the conversation, Burger left Athens, abruptly ending his visit before Georgia finished practice. "I literally started crying," Burger admitted. "I was hurt. I was embarrassed. But I tell you what, I never forgot that comment."

BURGER'S FEELINGS TOWARD GEORGIA only magnified in 1986. In his first season as a full-time starter, the redshirt junior had Auburn poised to win Dye's second conference title and first since 1983. Instead, as ten-and-a-half-point underdogs, unranked Georgia came to Jordan-Hare Stadium and stunned Auburn out of a possible championship. The deciding play came with less than a minute remaining, when Burger's pass was intercepted by linebacker Steve Boswell as Auburn marched toward a game-winning score.

"That loss stung so much," Burger said of the 20–16 defeat. "But give Georgia credit, they played great in '86. They deserved to win."

A year later, Auburn was again positioned to win Dye's second conference title. Only this time, Georgia wasn't an underdog. The No. 8 Bulldogs were 4-1 in conference play, and a victory over Auburn would clinch Dooley's seventh SEC crown and a trip to the Sugar Bowl. Sure, in his twenty-fourth season at Georgia, Dooley was used to playing for championships, but no starter on his 1987 roster had been in the same situation. As a reminder, Dooley hung a sign near Georgia's dressing room at Sanford Stadium. The banner read, "Be worthy as you run upon this hallowed sod. For you have dared to tread where Champions have trod."

For Auburn, what a difference a week made. Seven days before playing UGA, the Tigers suffered an embarrassing 34–6 home loss to Florida State University, dropping them from No. 6 to No. 12 in most national polls. In addition to the lopsided defeat, Auburn also lost All-American defensive lineman Tracy Rocker to a knee injury. However, despite losing to FSU, Auburn remained unbeaten in the SEC (3-0-1) and needed victories over UGA and Alabama to secure a conference title. "The week we played Georgia, that was the best week of practice we ever had," Burger said. "We came in Athens with a vengeance."

Sparked by Burger's arm, Auburn led 7–3 late in the second quarter before a perfect storm began to brew. After a Win Lyle field goal extended Auburn's

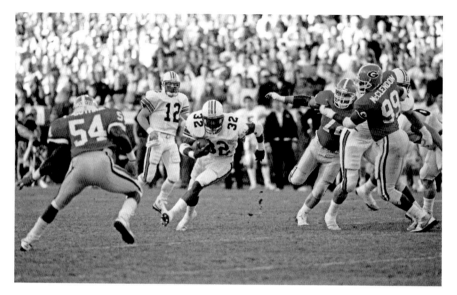

Jeff Burger (12) watches as Stacy Danley runs for a first down. *The* Augusta Chronicle.

halftime lead to 10–3, the Tigers opened the floodgates early in the third quarter. On its opening possession of the second half, Burger faced third and four on Auburn's thirty-nine-yard line when he found back Harry Mose open in the right flat. Fifty-five yards later, Mose was tackled on UGA's six-yard line. Three plays later, Burger hit receiver Duke Donaldson of Cairo, Georgia, for a touchdown: 17–3 Auburn.

With Georgia's Sugar Bowl dreams evaporating into the Athens air, the Bulldogs quarterback duo of James Jackson and Wayne Johnson sealed their own fate on UGA's ensuing two drives. Following Donaldson's touchdown, Jackson fumbled on Georgia's next possession, leading to another Lyle field goal (20–3 Auburn). Dooley then replaced Jackson with Johnson, who on his second play was intercepted by Auburn defensive lineman Nate Hill. One play later, Tigers receiver Alexander Wright found the end zone on a twenty-eight-yard reverse (27–3 Auburn).

"I was so nervous that I forgot our snap count," recalled Wright, now a pastor at Cornerstone Church in San Antonio, Texas. "Then I almost fumbled before I got going. Look, it worked out, but it could have been a disaster."

In all, Jackson and Johnson combined for four turnovers, while Burger completed twenty-two of thirty-two passes for 217 yards. As the Sanford Stadium clock ticked toward 0:00, Burger approached midfield as memories stormed back from his 1982 recruiting trip. The quarterback said eight words to Dooley: "Coach, never been scared of competition. Good game." Then, Burger had to answer to his head coach.

"Coach Dye was so confused," Burger said.

He grabbed me by the jersey and wanted to know what that was about. I told him, "It's a long story, but when Coach Dooley was recruiting me, he made the comment that if I was scared of competition then Georgia might not be the place for me." Coach Dye kind of chuckled. He told me, "I'm glad he said that."

THE MORNING AFTER THE GAME, *Athens Banner-Herald* assistant sports editor Charles Odom wrote a column titled, "Auburn Awakens Dogs from Sugary Dream." The article began by saying: "An old chant had been renewed this week around Bulldog country. It went something like—You can't spell Sugar without UGA. Instead, Sugar may rhyme somewhat with Burger."

Auburn went on to defeat Alabama, clinching Dye's second of four SEC pennants. The Tigers tied Syracuse in the Sugar Bowl. For Burger, however, it's not the 217 passing yards he remembers most about beating Georgia in Athens. It's what Larry Munson, UGA's legendary broadcaster, said during the broadcast. "My brother taped the game on our radio," Burger said. "I remember listening back and hearing Munson say, 'Well, guys, there's no question we've faced one of the premier passers in the SEC today in Jeff Burger.' Man, I got the biggest thrill from that. I was such a Larry Munson fan growing up and that meant the world to me."

Auburn's victory over UGA in 1987 tied the all-time series at 42-42-7.

INSIDE THE RIVALRY

Nearly twenty years after their handshake, Dooley and Burger crossed paths again—this time at Hartsfield-Jackson Atlanta Airport. In the early 2000s, both were invited to Nashville to film a Football Legends Reunion video, which were gaining popularity at many schools across the country. With the number of connections between Auburn and Georgia, video producers scheduled to film the institutions back-to-back, allowing Dooley and Dye to rightfully be in both productions. Also invited to be part of the Auburn Football Legends Reunion was Burger.

"So I go to Atlanta, get on a plane, and low-and-behold I'm sitting in first class next to Vince and Barbara Dooley," Burger said. "Coach Dooley couldn't have been nicer. I mean an absolute gentleman."

After arriving in Nashville, the Dooleys and Burger shared a limousine to the Grand Ole Opry Hotel, where filming took place. They shared a limousine back to Nashville International Airport and again sat together on the flight home to Georgia. The two spent hours side-by-side, yet neither mentioned the 1982 recruiting visit or 1987 postgame handshake.

"I wondered if Coach Dooley was going to bring it up," Burger admitted, "but he probably didn't think twice after it happened. Looking back, I know Coach Dooley's intentions weren't to offend me or anything like that. He just said it in the moment. I was only a teenager, you know? I took it a little more to heart."

21

THE COUNTDOWN GAME—1992

GEORGIA 14, AUBURN 10

The 1992 playing of the Deep South's Oldest Rivalry capped off a season-long celebration for Auburn and Georgia football. Each program was celebrating one hundred years of the sport, which started when the universities met in 1892 at Piedmont Park. Prior to the 1992 kickoff, representatives from both schools joined at midfield to exchange centennial footballs, while Auburn officials held the silver cup they were awarded for winning the inaugural contest. Following the ceremony, a coin commemorating the Deep South's Oldest Rivalry was used for the coin toss. The memento was flown into space (on shuttle flight *STS-53*) by astronaut Jim Voss, a 1972 Auburn University graduate.

PAT DYE'S FINAL HOME GAME as head coach was also his most bizarre. To this day, Auburn feels robbed of victory, haunted by the sight of Georgia coach Ray Goff violently motioning for his players to stay down. Trailing 14–10 on UGA's one-yard line, Auburn had nineteen seconds to score. More importantly, it had nineteen seconds to secure its sixth win.

"That game was pivotal because it would have assured us of making a bowl game," Auburn quarterback Stan White said. "Obviously, that didn't happen."

With victory inches away, a timeout was called, allowing Auburn to decide which play to run. The first option was a quarterback sneak with White. Option two: A fullback dive to James Bostic over left guard. "James was lobbying to get it," White remembered. "So we went with that call."

Stan White attempts a pass over the outstretched arms of UGA defensive end Phillip Daniels (89). *Morris Communications.*

Being second down, Auburn—despite having no timeouts—felt confident that even if Bostic didn't score there would be ample time to clock the football on third down and have a final play to decide the outcome. Instead, mayhem ensued. During the timeout, while deliberating between a sneak by White or a handoff to Bostic, fellow Auburn tailback Joe Frazier confused his blocking assignment for the play. Instead of blocking Georgia's defensive end, which was Frazier's job on a run by Bostic, Frazier ran straight ahead as if he was going to push White from behind on a quarterback sneak. When White turned to give to Bostic, he was met by Frazier.

"We fumbled but it didn't take long to determine James had the ball," White said. "Once it was clear that James recovered, we went to line up and clock the thing. Look, nineteen seconds is an eternity. The play itself had only taken about three."

As Auburn raced to reorganize, Georgia was in no hurry to do the same. Knowing the clock was running, UGA players laid on the Jordan-Hare Stadium turf in hopes that time would expire.

"Before the play, we didn't tell our guys to stay down or anything," Goff said. "I wish I could say I was smart enough to think of that. Our players did it on their own."

The referees never whistled to seize the chaos, and when Auburn was finally able to line up to take its third-down snap, there was one significant problem. "I went to take the snap and my center reaches up and goes, 'We don't have the football,'" White recalled. "A Georgia defender had kicked it away."

With no rule in place to prevent defenders from committing a delay of game penalty, the clock continued to tick. And tick. And tick. Before Auburn could take another snap, nineteen seconds had vanished. Dogs win.

"I was furious," White remembered. "I went and grabbed the head official as he ran off the field. I said, 'This is wrong! They kicked the ball, they kicked it! You have to put more time on the clock!'"

Stunned by what they'd witnessed, the first sellout crowd at Jordan-Hare Stadium since playing UGA in 1990 refused to leave. Thousands stayed. And not just for a couple of minutes. For what seemed like hours, Auburn faithful waited for officials to reappear to add time to an ending that, in their mind, was ripped away. At one point, even Goff stopped walking toward Georgia's locker room as if he believed the game might not be over. "Oh, I knew it was over," Goff said in 2016. "Once those officials left, they weren't coming back out."

John Spagnola was broadcasting the game for ABC and said, "[The fans] are in stunned silence and they're not leaving. Nobody's leaving. They want the officials to rectify this thing and I really have to question what happened there with the officiating."

In the end, 14–10 stood. Enraged by the ruling, Auburn fans showered their end zones with litter, marking an unfortunate end to Dye's twelve-year tenure on the Plains. UGA tailback Garrison Hearst didn't take kindly to the trash-throwing, saying after the game, "I don't understand fans like that. That's low-class people. I don't want to play here again because of the fans. [Auburn players] were great. They played fairly. You get out here and you have to deal with the fans more than you do the team."

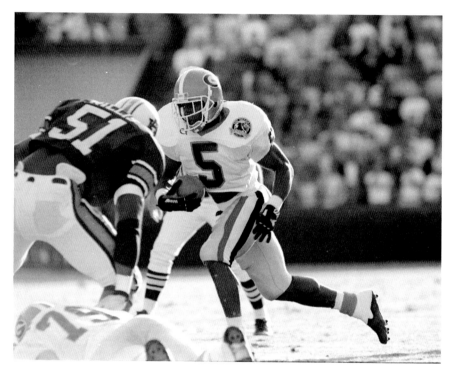

Garrison Hearst carries the ball against Auburn. *Morris Communications.*

Georgia's Defense Stands Tall

When Mitch Davis looks back on the 1992 Auburn-Georgia game, the former linebacker and native of Mobile, Alabama, uses six words to describe the final nineteen seconds: "God finally looked down on us."

Earlier in the season, UGA suffered a pair of gut-wrenching losses: 34–31 to Tennessee and 26–24 to Florida. The defeats prevented Georgia from competing for an SEC championship, while leaving Davis to question why his team was twice on the wrong end of coin-flip outcomes.

"Those losses hurt so bad," Davis said. "To this day, players from our 1992 team annually get together and we always talk about being five points shy of a championship. For me, the one that hurt most was Tennessee. I put a lot of blame on myself for that game because I went out in the fourth quarter. I was exhausted. Well, Tennessee ran right at my replacement and scored a touchdown."

UGA players celebrate as head coach Ray Goff nervously awaits the outcome of the 1992 game at Auburn. *Morris Communications.*

Nine weeks after losing to Tennessee, UGA's defense was having déjà-vu at Jordan-Hare Stadium. Despite holding Auburn to ten points through fifty-nine minutes, the Tigers were effortlessly moving on their final drive. "We couldn't stop them," Davis admitted. "We were dead tired and there was nothing we could do about it. About midway through Auburn's last drive, I said to myself, 'Lord, please don't let this happen again. I can't take another loss like this.'"

Auburn's offense had gone forty-four yards in 2:17, marching its way to Georgia's one-yard line before a timeout was called with nineteen seconds left. While Auburn designed a run to Bostic, UGA defensive coordinator Richard Bell told his unit to pinch down and collapse inside.

"We were in trouble if Auburn went outside," Davis said, "but they played right into our defense. We were hoping they'd run up the middle and that's exactly what they did."

Davis was blocked at the line of scrimmage before realizing the ball was on the ground. At that point, he did everything possible to not have to play another down. "I started grabbing their players and pulling them down with me," Davis said. "We had to make nineteen seconds disappear. Look, we were beyond exhausted and if Auburn was able to run another play they would have won that ballgame."

The Tigers never got the opportunity. As the game clock dwindled to 0:00, the star linebacker from Vigor High School sprinted toward UGA's student section.

"I'll never forget jumping into our stands," Davis said.

Mitch Davis puts pressure on Stan White. *Morris Communications.*

Man, that was the best feeling ever. I turned around and had about six cameras in my face. I guess everyone wanted an interview because I was from Alabama, so I start talking to reporters and then notice my teammates running to the locker room with hands over their head. Those Auburn fans were throwing everything on the field. By the time I went in, I was running with a police officer and we were both holding our heads for protection.

INSIDE THE RIVALRY

Nine years after what Georgia coined "The Countdown Game," it was the Bulldogs' turn at disaster. Facing nearly the identical situation as Auburn had in 1992, the 2001 Dogs had driven to the two-yard line with sixteen seconds to play at Sanford Stadium. In Mark Richt's first season in Athens, the coach called a handoff to tailback Jasper Sanks, who was bulldozed at the line of scrimmage. Now frantic on the sideline, Richt signaled for a timeout. He didn't have one. He motioned for freshman quarterback David Greene to spike the ball. There wasn't enough time. As Georgia faithful unanimously thought, "Why did we run the ball?" the clock struck 0:00.

Auburn won, 24–17.

22

THE TIE THAT CRUSHED AUBURN—1994

GEORGIA 23, AUBURN 23

Auburn finished with an 11-0 record in 1993 and was 9-0 in 1994 leading up to the Deep South's Oldest Rivalry. Neither Auburn team, however, was eligible to compete for the SEC championship or bowl game due to NCAA sanctions after an investigation revealed booster Corky Frost had made illicit payments to defensive back Eric Ramsey. In spite of the 1994

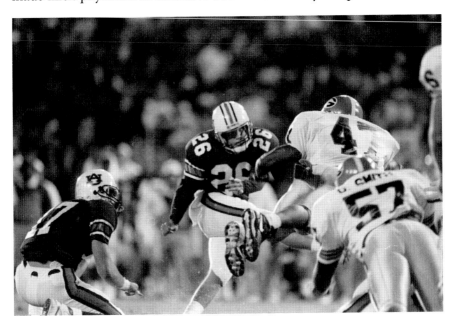

Auburn kicker Matt Hawkins misses a potential game-winning field goal against UGA.
Morris Communications.

postseason ban, Auburn still had an outside chance to be crowned national champions with wins over Georgia and Alabama. That dream, however, was shattered on November 12.

LESS THAN TWENTY-FOUR HOURS AFTER leaving Jordan-Hare Stadium, Matt Hawkins rose from his pew on November 13, 1994, as the congregation began singing "I Exalt Thee." Like every Sunday, Auburn's junior kicker had woken up early to worship at Lakeview Baptist Church on East Glenn Avenue.

"About the second chorus, I couldn't sing any longer," Hawkins said. "So I left the sanctuary, went into the Sunday school room and cried for an hour. By the time I composed myself the service was over."

The night before, Hawkins was given an opportunity he had always dreamed of: a field goal to decide a game. A successful kick would've extended Auburn's win streak to twenty-one games and kept alive hopes of a national title. Instead, the twenty-one-year-old pushed the attempt right, leading to Auburn's first letdown under head coach Terry Bowden. "As I walked off the field I just asked God, 'Why?'" Hawkins said. "But God has a plan for everything, including what happens in football for an individual's life. That was his plan for me."

For Auburn fans, much of the blame was immediately directed toward Hawkins, but he wasn't the only one at fault. The No. 3 Tigers led 23–9 late in the third quarter before the defense relinquished a seventy-nine-yard touchdown pass from Eric Zeier to Juan Daniels. The defense allowed the game-tying score on UGA's opening drive of the fourth quarter. Making matters worse for the home team, Auburn's offense went scoreless during the final 26:58 against a defense that had suffered embarrassing losses to Vanderbilt (43–30 on homecoming), Tennessee (41–23) and Florida (52–14).

"Most people don't remember what the offense and defense did," Hawkins said. "No one looks back and thinks of us blowing that two-touchdown lead. I tell you what, though, everyone remembers my kick."

After the game, Hawkins went back to his dorm room, which he shared with quarterback Patrick Nix. On their answering machine were seven messages. "The first three were anonymous people cussing me out," Hawkins recalled. "The next four were friends of mine who were praying and encouraging me."

During his postgame interview, Hawkins had quoted Bible scripture to members of the media, and some of his quotes landed in newspaper articles the following morning.

"The next week, I received about eighty letters of encouragement from people all over the country," Hawkins said. "I got more letters in those seven days than my entire football career combined. It truly meant a lot to read what people had to say and know my trials were impacting others."

Hawkins, who struggles from a speech impediment, received notes from two kids who also stuttered. Some cards came from pastors, telling Hawkins they used his quotes as part of their Sunday sermons. Even an Applebee's waiter wrote to express appreciation.

"Most importantly, that kick taught me about trials," Hawkins said. "There's a significance when you can approach someone who's going through a trial and say, 'Hey, I've had dreams before, too, and I lost them in front of a million people on TV and 87,000 in the stands.'"

After graduation, Hawkins stayed in Auburn, where he was a youth pastor for eleven years. He now lives in Ripley, Tennessee, and is a senior pastor at First Baptist Church.

"This was God's plan and he used my experience against Georgia over and over again in people's lives," Hawkins said. "He enabled me to administer to others through a silly kick one Saturday night in November. As much as it crushed me that week, I've come to understand it was only a kick."

JUAN DANIELS

More than a decade before silencing Jordan-Hare Stadium with his seventy-nine-yard touchdown reception, Juan Daniels arrived at a small Albany, Georgia cemetery on August 25, 1983. Daniels, eight years old at the time, was there to lay his hero to rest.

Throughout his childhood, Daniels would often visit Albany to see Greg Pratt, his first cousin. Pratt, the five-foot, eight-inch, 211-pound fullback, helped pave the way for Bo Jackson, Randy Campbell, Lionel James and the rest of Auburn's star-studded backfield during the 1982 season. He was Auburn's projected starter leading up to 1983. However, while trying to complete the last of a series of 440-yard dashes, Pratt collapsed and died on an Auburn practice field seventeen days before the start of the 1983 season.

"He was my hero," Daniels said. "To this day, Greg Pratt's still my hero. I have his letterman's jacket. I have every Auburn clipping. Anything Auburn you can imagine, I have it."

Juan Daniels is pulled down after making a catch against Auburn in 1994. *Morris Communications.*

Before Pratt's death, Daniels would sneak into the fullback's Albany bedroom and take Auburn T-shirts from his dresser drawer. The seven-year-old would wear them to school the next week, claiming, "I thought I was the coolest kid ever." Even after Pratt's passing, Daniels continued his Auburn obsession, choosing to wear No. 14 at Norcross High School to emulate Tigers quarterback Randy Campbell.

"My senior year at Norcross, my entire room was Auburn," Daniels admitted. "It was insane how much I loved them. I had this blown-up picture of Bo Jackson in a Superman outfit and he's coming out of a telephone booth. No one loved Auburn more than I did."

For Daniels, his senior year also occurred during arguably the most tumultuous twelve-month span in Auburn football history. In 1992, the future of Coach Dye was put in question as the NCAA investigated the school for improper benefits. Dye still recruited Daniels, but he was up front with the wide receiver prospect.

Coach Dye told me, "Juan, I'm gonna be honest with you. The likelihood of me being at Auburn next year   isn't too good. It probably isn't going to happen." Then Coach Dye told me about Georgia. He said, "Juan, Georgia's my alma mater and they have a great program there. I just want to be honest with you so you can make an informed decision."

Despite his love for Auburn, Daniels elected to stay in state and play for Ray Goff at UGA. Unfortunately for his childhood love, Daniels's dream of making a game-changing play at Jordan-Hare Stadium came true in 1994. Trailing 23–9 with 4:15 remaining in the third quarter, Georgia faced first and ten at its own twenty-one-yard line.

"When we called the play, it was originally a running play," Daniels remembered. "It was called 55, which was an off-tackle run away from the tight end. So we weren't even supposed to pass, but when we got to the line of scrimmage, [UGA quarterback Eric] Zeier noticed we had single coverage on the outside and he checked to give me a post."

Added Zeier: "Auburn was playing a quarters look and we had an in-route to occupy the safety and had Juan going over the top with a post. We got exactly the look we wanted."

Zeier hit Daniels in stride, and the second-string receiver outran Auburn's secondary for a seventy-nine-yard score. Suddenly, UGA was back in the game.

"[Zeier] came up and put his hands around my helmet," Daniels recalled. "He said, 'That's a big play! That's a big play!'"

Less than six minutes after Daniels's touchdown, UGA scored again when Zeier hit a four-yard strike to Brice Hunter. Kanon Parkman converted the extra point to even the contest at 23–23. Neither team scored during the final 13:06.

"Look, the scoreboard said it was a tie, but we were celebrating," Daniels said.

We lost 52–14 to Florida the game before playing Auburn, while Auburn had beaten Florida in Gainesville earlier that season. I'll never forget, Coach Goff said to us after the game, "Men, this is the team we were supposed to be. This is the team we were supposed to be all season." He was right, too. We had a star quarterback, Terrell Davis at running back, Brice Hunter, Hines Ward, Robert Edwards. I mean, we had an All-Star cast but never put it all together until that second half at Auburn.

Daniels graduated from Georgia following the 1996 season and met his wife during his time in Athens. The couple has three children who pull for UGA. However, despite never donning orange and blue, Daniels's love for Auburn remains.

"I love Georgia," the wide receiver said. "I still love Auburn, too. I have a house-divided license plate on my car and a big piece of my heart remains with Auburn. You know, it's crazy how life works out. I don't regret going to Georgia but Auburn will always be my first love. When Auburn won the 2010 national championship, I screamed so loud the entire house woke up."

23

LEARD TO DANIELS—1999

AUBURN 38, GEORGIA 21

For Ben Leard, it was personal. For Ronney Daniels, it was perfect. For both, November 13, 1999, remains the most prolific second quarter in the history of the Deep South's Oldest Rivalry.

"Nothing topped going home that year for Thanksgiving," said Leard, a native of Hartwell, Georgia.

Leard quarterbacked Hart County High from 1992 to 1995 and was recruited by UGA beginning his sophomore season. Head coach Ray Goff wanted him. As did offensive coordinator Greg Davis. For two years, Davis stayed in touch with Leard, even visiting the quarterback's home. That ended, however, when Goff and his staff were let go on November 15, 1995.

"I thought the world of Coach Davis," said Leard, who was a senior when the firings occurred. "That decision changed everything for me. I'm not saying I would've committed to Georgia if Coach Davis never left, but I would've strongly considered it."

Despite the change in leadership, Leard still visited Athens to meet new head coach Jim Donnan. The chemistry, however, wasn't there. "I just didn't click with Jim Donnan," Leard said. "So I made the best decision, and that was Auburn."

Leard's choice, however, didn't stop critics from questioning his reasons.

"A lot of people said I picked Auburn because Georgia didn't want me," Leard said. "That's a complete misnomer. Look, as an Auburn player, you want to first and foremost beat Alabama. But on a scale of 1 to 100, if beating Alabama is 100, my desire to beat Georgia was 99.999."

Ronney Daniels (25) catches a touchdown pass in 1999 at Sanford Stadium. *Morris Communications.*

On November 13, 1999, Leard got his chance. With friends and family in attendance, the Hart County native shredded No. 14 Georgia to the tune of 416 yards (setting a school record) and four touchdowns (tying a school record). Every touchdown pass came in the first two quarters, propelling unranked Auburn to a 31-0 halftime lead, as a chorus of boos rained down on Sanford Stadium. Leard's main beneficiary was freshman receiver Ronney Daniels. With Georgia's defense focused on stopping the run, Daniels had five catches for 161 yards and two touchdowns—in the second quarter alone.

"Every touchdown Ronney caught was called off an audible," Leard said. "It was never the play called in the huddle but we saw exactly what we wanted in the way Georgia lined up."

Each time the junior quarterback saw a favorable matchup, Leard tapped his equipment, cueing Daniels to adjust his route. Each time, Daniels returned a signal to Leard, showing his quarterback he understood. The ball never touched the ground. First, Daniels beat UGA senior cornerback Jeff Harris for a fifty-nine-yard score down the left sideline. The freshman then outran Cory Robinson for a seventy-eight-yard touchdown.

"After my first touchdown, Ben ran up and yelled, 'Even if they start doubling you, I'm going your way. I'm going your way all night,'" Daniels remembered. "I just looked back and said, 'I got you, Ben.'"

On Auburn's opening drive of the third quarter, Leard and Daniels teamed up again, this time for a fifty-seven-yard completion. The play moved Auburn to Georgia's three-yard line. Two plays later, Leard scored on a quarterback sneak to make it 38–0. "You know that walkway at Sanford Stadium that goes behind our bench?" Daniels asked, rhetorically. "Man, their fans flooded out early and were yelling all sorts of things my direction. I loved it. I mean, I absolutely loved it."

As the banter continued, Daniels finally turned around, looked toward the famed hedges and asked UGA faithful a simple question.

"'Where y'all going?' That's exactly what I asked them," Daniels said. "They kept saying, 'You suck 25, You suck 25,' so I gave them a thumbs-up and said, 'Please don't leave, I still have one more left!'"

Daniels wasn't the only recipient of choice words from UGA fans. Auburn first-year offensive line coach Hugh Nall, a member of Georgia's 1980 national championship team, also received an earful.

"Some of the worst chew-outs I ever got were from people across the hedges," Nall said. "I'd look back and go, 'You really don't know who you're talking to.'"

For the Hart County native, it was his only career start at Sanford Stadium, and it almost didn't happen. In late September, Leard separated his shoulder against Ole Miss, causing him to miss four weeks. He returned October 30 against Arkansas but was forced to leave with a concussion. Auburn went 1-4 in 1999 without Leard. It was Tommy Tuberville's first year as head coach.

"I was rusty starting our week of preparation for Georgia," Leard admitted.

But we got really sharp as the week went on. I'll never forget our Friday walkthrough—our offense connected perfectly. We stayed in Gwinnett on Friday night, took back roads through Commerce on Saturday, then came up behind Sanford Stadium before kickoff. I had a feeling something special would happen.

An article by Jay G. Tate of the *Montgomery Advertiser* stated:

Auburn supposedly had no business beating Georgia Saturday night. The Bulldogs have established themselves as one of the conference's best teams. They have sophomore quarterback Quincy Carter, who is good. They have a powerful running game, which is very good. They have a brutal defense which ranks as one of the conference's most stingy. All good. But Auburn, not dissuaded with a 4-5 record going into the game, had something UGA didn't have Saturday. The Tigers, for the first time in months, had a healthy Ben Leard.

Looking back on the victory, Leard and Daniels are quick to praise offensive coordinator Noel Mazzone, who stressed all week that Georgia would dare his unit to beat them through the air. Leard did exactly that. But it's his rushing score that remains enshrined on his living room wall.

"One of the best gifts I ever received was from my cousin's husband, a UGA photographer named Andy Tucker," Leard said. "He took a photo as I'm coming through the line of scrimmage to make it 38–0. Man, it's one of my favorite keepsakes ever."

Tucker credits the gift as a key spark in landing a date with his future wife, Amy Leard Tucker. "I had to get in good with the family," said Tucker, laughing. "I gave Ben that photo in November 1999, and Amy and I went on our first date that December. It's safe to say that photo played a big role in her agreeing to date me."

For Daniels, he simply remembers the game as Auburn's coming-out party.

"It was the coming-out party for all of us," Daniels said. "Me, Ben, Coach Tubs—everybody. All year, Coach Tubs wanted to prove we could play with anyone in the SEC, and we accomplished that by beating Georgia."

Auburn finished the year 5-6 and failed to make a bowl game. No. 16 Georgia went 8-4, capped by an Outback Bowl victory over Purdue.

"I have two favorite games during my career at Auburn," Leard said. "Beating Alabama [in 2000] to win the SEC West, and what we did that night at Sanford Stadium. I'll never forget either one."

24

THE NIGHT ODELL OWNED ATHENS—2003

GEORGIA 26, AUBURN 7

Throughout April 2016, my goal was to track down Odell Thurman. I reached out to his hometown athletic director, newspaper reporters and even former coaches. No one had a phone number. No one knew an address. So on the last day of April, I turned west on Interstate 20 and eventually landed at a middle school baseball field in Jasper County, Georgia.

From 2003 to 2016, Thurman's story was littered with highs and lows. Some moments too perfect to script. Others too painful to forget. A kid from Monticello, Georgia, raised by his grandmother, Betty Thurman, and forced to share a home with an uncle, aunt and seven cousins. A kid who lost his

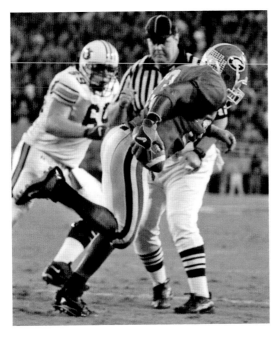

Odell Thurman returns an interception ninety-nine yards for a touchdown to seal Georgia's 2003 victory over Auburn. *Morris Communications.*

mother, Joyce Bland, in a car wreck when he was ten. He lost his father ten years later.

On August 23, 2003, all but one University of Georgia football player signed autographs and posed for pictures at UGA's annual Fan Day. Odell was in Monticello, burying his forty-one-year-old father, who had died from liver and kidney failure. Otis Thurman passed away eight days before his son's first game in red and black.

Having missed practice to lay his father to rest, Odell didn't start the 2003 season-opener against Clemson but still tallied four tackles and a quarterback hurry in Georgia's 30–0 victory. From that point on, Thurman gradually became a star on a defense littered with playmakers—Thomas Davis, David Pollack, Sean Jones, Greg Blue, Tim Jennings. On November 1, 2003, Thurman was the centerpiece of *Dawg Post Magazine*, as three words were printed across his chest: The Monticello Monster.

Everything was pointing toward the Deep South's Oldest Rivalry.

April 30, 2016

As I approached Monticello's baseball field, every player and coach was wearing purple. A seventh-grader named Graham took batting practice, while a pair of coaches taught him how to bunt. Standing at Monticello Middle School, it was hard not to think about Odell Thurman. This town is where it all started, where Odell became Odell. The high school football field sits a short distance away, where Thurman was named *Macon Telegraph* All-State before committing to UGA in 2000. By many accounts, he was Jasper County's most sought-after talent since Trisha Yearwood.

In town, some still spoke fondly about him, recalling his parade on the town square after being drafted by the Cincinnati Bengals in April 2005. Many say his name in disappointment, a sense of what might have been after repeated suspensions for substance abuse by NFL commissioner Roger Goodell. During a water break at baseball practice, I asked a coach if he had any way of contacting Thurman. Like everyone else I reached out to, he had no phone number or e-mail. But he did remember an address on a winding road behind Monticello's courthouse where Odell grew up. "We call that area Frog Town," the coach said. "If Odell's in Monticello, that's where he'll be."

AUBURN AT GEORGIA, NOVEMBER 15, 2003

Thursday night before the 2003 Auburn-Georgia game, Thurman sat downstairs at Flanagan's Bar in downtown Athens. With two teammates beside him, I approached the table, wished Thurman luck and jokingly made a proposition. "When you make the game-winning interception, I want those No. 33 gloves." Like he always did, Thurman smiled, laughed, shook my hand and said, "You got it."

Forty-eight hours later, Thurman and the rest of Georgia's defense were in the middle of another dominating performance. Through the first nine games of 2003, Georgia's unit was holding opponents to 10.8 points per game and hadn't relinquished more than 20 points in a contest since October 4. The Deep South's Oldest Rivalry was no different. At halftime, Auburn's offense totaled fifty-four yards. After three quarters, the Tigers remained shutout, hardly having sniffed Georgia's side of the fifty. But with 11:31 remaining in the fourth quarter, the visitors were threatening. Despite trailing 19–0 after three periods, Auburn was in the midst of a seven-play drive and faced third and goal from Georgia's two-yard line. Lining up in an empty backfield, Auburn quarterback Jason Campbell

Odell Thurman dives for a tackle on Auburn quarterback Jason Campbell. *Morris Communications.*

received the snap, was flushed right and then threw across his body toward Carnell "Cadillac" Williams.

After a deflection by UGA linebacker Tony Taylor, the ball inched toward Sanford Stadium's grass when, seemingly out of nowhere, Thurman darted from three yards deep in the end zone and hauled in the interception. Over the next thirteen seconds, Odell Thurman sprinted into Auburn-Georgia lore. With 92,058 (mostly UGA) fans shaking Sanford Stadium, Thurman went ninety-nine-yards to the opposite end zone to end any hope of an Auburn comeback. The win marked UGA's first home victory over the Tigers since 1991.

As the game wound down, I left Section 140 and walked toward the hedges near a slew of celebrating players. The moment Odell saw me, he slid off both gloves and tossed them in my direction. "I didn't forget," he shouted.

The following week, UGA defensive coordinator Brian VanGorder gave Thurman negative grades on the play for poor technique and for being out of position. Like much of Thurman's football career, even when he was right, he was somehow in the wrong.

APRIL 30, 2016

The front of Odell Thurman's childhood home looked modest, with a grassy yard and a basketball goal near the driveway. The backyard had two trash barrels and a worn-out RV behind the residence. A child's tricycle lay in the driveway, tilted on its side.

Unaware if anyone was home, I knocked twice on the side door when a relative of Thurman answered.

"Odell isn't here right now," said Jessie Gude, shaking my hand. "Why do you wanna see my cousin?"

I told Gude I was writing a book on the Deep South's Oldest Rivalry and was hoping to speak with Thurman about the game in 2003. Once I mentioned "2003 Auburn-Georgia," it was like a light bulb flashed on. That game. That interception. Everything about November 15, 2003, is still remembered on the streets of Frog Town. Quite frankly, it was Odell Thurman's finest football moment. "Man, you wanna know about *The Play*?" Gude asked, now excited. "I'm telling you, my cousin was a hero that night."

I handed Gude my business card, at which time he reached down with both hands as if he was about to lift a plant from the porch. But there was no plant. Instead, he was imitating Thurman's interception.

"Just like that," Gude said before pausing. "Hang on real quick. Odell has a card, too."

Gude went inside then reappeared with a stack of 2006 Upper Deck football cards. On the card is Thurman, wearing white gloves, making an interception for the Cincinnati Bengals. "Here's one for you," Gude said.

With card No. 42 in hand, I left Monticello. Odell Thurman never called.

25

THE HIT—2004

AUBURN 24, GEORGIA 6

*The 2004 matchup marked the first time both programs were ranked in the
top five since facing each other in 1983. Similar to '83, Auburn defeated the
Bulldogs and eventually captured the SEC championship.*

Unsure of Reggie Brown's condition, Junior Rosegreen took a knee and
prayed on the field at Jordan-Hare Stadium.

Reggie Brown was knocked unconscious during the 2004 game at Auburn. *Morris Communications.*

"Lord, this is a game we all love and no one deserves to go down doing what they love. If it's Your will, please let Reggie Brown get back up," said Rosegreen, moments after striking Georgia's wide receiver.

Brown was diagnosed with a concussion but suffered no spinal or neck injuries. More than a decade later, what's known as "The Hit" has more than fourteen million YouTube views and remains one of the most recognized collisions in college football history.

"I coach defensive backs at Boyd Anderson High School [Florida], and my kids always come up and say, 'Coach, I watched that video and I wanna hit just like you,'" Rosegreen said in 2015. "I tell them, 'No. Be better than me.'"

During Rosegreen's career on the Plains, arguably his most coveted trait was an ability to play with passion. No game was bigger than the other, whether it was opening his senior year against Louisiana-Monroe or capping an undefeated season in the Sugar Bowl. But after a phone conversation the morning of the 2004 Auburn-Georgia game, Rosegreen had extra incentive to make his final home game his most memorable. In the moments before leaving Auburn's team hotel, Rosegreen received a call from his family, as crying voices were heard on the other end. At ninety-nine years old, the safety's grandmother had passed away.

"Right then, I wanted to do something great for my grandma," Rosegreen said. "I wanted to lay everything on the line for her that day."

The motivation only amplified when Rosegreen arrived at Jordan-Hare Stadium. During warmups, UGA receiver Fred Gibson was trash-talking with Auburn cornerback, and longtime friend, Carlos Rogers before Rogers motioned Rosegreen to join their conversation. Standing feet apart, Gibson warned Rogers and Rosegreen that he planned to score on both defensive backs and end their perfect season.

"Fred Gibson was trash talking like you wouldn't believe," Rosegreen said. "He kept saying, 'Rosegreen, I'm gonna do this to you. Rosegreen, I'm gonna do that to you.' I took it very personal."

As Gibson and Rogers kept talking, Rosegreen's emotions expanded. Having already dedicated the game to his grandmother, Rosegreen took each of Gibson's comments to heart to the point where the safety was ready to implode—and this was pregame warmups. "I wanted to take Fred Gibson's head off," Rosegreen said. "In Fred's defense though, he didn't know my grandma had passed that morning. He didn't know the kind of chip I had on my shoulder. Still, someone had to pay for his trash talking."

That someone proved to be Reggie Brown. With 7:06 left in the third quarter, Brown ran a seam route, cut toward Rosegreen, and Georgia quarterback David Greene fired in his direction. Almost instantly after receiving the pass, Rosegreen's helmet collided with Brown's head, knocking the ball loose and causing the receiver to lay motionless at Auburn's eleven-yard line.

"Right after the hit, I was so jacked up that I didn't even think about Reggie Brown," Rosegreen admitted. "But when I ran to the side, that's when I realized he might be dead. You know, he wasn't moving but he was doing this vibrating motion. At that point, I just prayed. All I wanted was for [Reggie Brown] to get up."

As Brown stayed still, a section of Georgia fans in the north end zone began chanting "Reggie." Auburn fans soon joined the chant, as echoes of "Reg-gie" could be heard throughout Jordan-Hare Stadium. The morning after the game, Charles Shepard of the *Athens Banner-Herald* wrote, "A helmet-to-helmet collision left Georgia receiver Reggie Brown motionless on the ground Saturday, but united 87,451 of the South's most bitter rivals."

REGGIE BROWN LOOKS BACK ON "THE HIT"

Reggie Brown remembers running the seam route. He recalls heading in the direction of Junior Rosegreen. After that, it's a blur. "The only thing I remember is being in an ambulance with our trainer," Brown said. "At that point I knew. I mean, there was no other reason why I'd be in an ambulance. I just looked at him and said, 'I must've gotten knocked out, huh?'"

As vicious as Rosegreen's hit was, Brown, a Carrollton, Georgia native, was cleared to ride home with UGA's team after the game. The following Monday, Rosegreen reached out to Brown, calling to check on the wide receiver.

"Rosegreen kept apologizing and I was like, 'There's nothing to be sorry about,'" Brown said. "Then he said, 'That hit was supposed to be for Fred Gibson.' I got a pretty good laugh about that."

For Brown, despite being asked about the play countless times, the receiver went years without watching a replay. In Brown's words, "Why watch it when I lived it?" Eventually, however, temptation proved too much. Of the fourteen million YouTube views, one was finally added by Brown himself.

"Right when I clicked the link, music starts playing to the beat of the play," Brown said. "I thought, 'Really? The hit wasn't good enough by itself?' But, yeah, it was about like I expected."

Despite not being upset with Rosegreen, Brown admits he was disappointed with the play call—a route that left him unprotected in the middle of the field. Throughout the 2004 season, Brown says he and Gibson both voiced displeasure over the play and feared that it could lead to a serious injury.

After his collision in Auburn, Brown never ran the route again.

"We'd be in the film room and Fred and I both worried about that play," Brown said. "We didn't like it at all. Fortunately, the hit at Auburn wasn't nearly as bad as it looked."

In 2004, there was no targeting penalty, but the hit played a large role in initiating a rule to further protect wide receivers. In August 2005, Brown's rookie season with the Philadelphia Eagles, the NCAA strengthened its spearing penalty to remove any reference to intent. (The previous rule only penalized players who intentionally led with their helmet, forcing officials to judge whether a deliberate strike was made.) Georgia athletic trainer Ron Courson, who tended to Brown while he was lying motionless, headed a task force to initiate the rule change.

"THAT HIT WAS SUPPOSED TO BE FOR FRED GIBSON"

Fred Gibson finished the 2004 season with forty-nine receptions for 801 yards and seven touchdowns. None of those statistics came November 13 against Auburn. With defensive coordinator Gene Chizik focused on shutting down Georgia's top target, Gibson was held to zero catches for the only time his senior year.

"That whole game they played Cover 2 against me," Gibson said. "I was never left one-on-one. Look, it was a great game plan and I can flat-out say we got our ass whipped. Auburn whipped our ass. That team was national champions if you ask me."

Although Gibson didn't create noise statistically, his impact was clearly felt on the game. Gibson, from Waycross, Georgia, and Carlos Rogers, of Augusta, had been friends during high school and talked numerous times leading up to the showdown between No. 5 Georgia and No. 3 Auburn. "One thing about Carlos Rogers is he's always joking around," Gibson said. "He's a jokester."

Before kickoff, Gibson admits to trash-talking, but he says Rogers is responsible for keeping Rosegreen fired up throughout the contest.

"Look, I didn't know Rosegreen and Rosegreen didn't know me," Gibson said. "Carlos, he wanted to beat Georgia so bad that he was feeding Rosegreen all these lies to keep hyping that man up. It worked, too. Rosegreen wanted to kill me on that field. Rosegreen was playing like the No. 1 pick in the NFL draft."

Rosegreen and Rogers combined for twelve tackles, while Rogers also added a sack and interception. Rosegreen tallied a forced fumble for his hit on Brown. After Auburn's 24–6 statement victory, it didn't take long for Gibson's phone to ring.

"Of course Carlos calls and starts laughing," Gibson said. "That's his main thing—he laughs a lot. Carlos just said, 'Boy, I told you. I told you!'"

Auburn finished 2004 with a 13-0 record but was left out of the BCS Championship Game in favor of Southern California and Oklahoma. In honor of going unbeaten, Tigers coach Tommy Tuberville still awarded each player with a national championship ring.

26

BATTLE WINS THIS WAR—2006

GEORGIA 37, AUBURN 15

Taviana, my older sister, went to Auburn and I hated giving her a ticket to that game. She'd sit in the Georgia family section, all dressed up in orange and blue, wearing a tiny UGA button that said, "I support 25."
—Tra Battle, Georgia safety.

Preparing for an 11:00 a.m. kickoff, Tra Battle sat at his locker in the visitors' dressing room of Jordan-Hare Stadium on November 11, 2006. Coach Mark Richt had long since disallowed players from listening to headphones before kickoff, but this day was different. Battle needed to hear something. So the senior snuck out his iPhone, didn't say a word and quietly etched his focus

Members of UGA's secondary, Greg Blue (17), Tra Battle (25) and Kelin Johnson (30) agonize after losing to Auburn in 2005. Battle would get revenge on the Tigers a year later. *Morris Communications.*

through music. "I wanted redemption," Battle said. "I felt responsible for that loss in 2005—a loss that took us out of the national title hunt."

A YEAR EARLIER, IN 2005 AT SANFORD STADIUM, Battle was in Georgia's secondary when Auburn quarterback Brandon Cox connected with Devin Aromashodu on fourth and ten with 2:05 remaining. With Auburn trailing 30–28, Aromashodu ran sixty-three yards before UGA defensive back Paul Oliver knocked the ball loose, sending it squirming into Georgia's end zone.

"Years later, me and Courtney Taylor were talking about that play in 2005," said Auburn linebacker Karibi Dede. "C.T. looked at me and goes, 'I was running so fast because I wanted to be in the newspaper. I wanted to be on the front page celebrating with Devin.'"

Taylor added: "I'll admit it: The main reason I was chasing Devin so hard was to be in the Sunday paper. I wanted to get in that celebration shot." Instead, Taylor became the headline. With the ball inches from being a touchback (likely ending the game), Taylor pounced on the fumble, and Auburn retained possession. Three plays later, John Vaughn kicked the game-winning chip shot, and No. 15 Auburn upset No. 9 UGA, 31–30.

"I still look back on that play for motivation," Taylor said. "It taught me not to give up because you never know what'll happen next. Aside from my touchdown against LSU [in 2004], recovering that fumble at Georgia was the greatest play of my Auburn career. I truly rank those two plays 1A and 1B."

UGA senior Tra Battle fully extends himself over the goal line. *John Kelley.*

Georgia, despite falling to Florida and Auburn, still won the 2005 SEC championship, but Battle hadn't forgotten that night. That play. That heartbreaking loss Between the Hedges.

"For an entire year I thought about redeeming myself," Battle said. "That loss to Auburn hurt so bad. I couldn't stop reliving that play."

BEFORE UNDERSTANDING BATTLE'S URGE for redemption, it's important to note his beginning. Unlike most UGA defenders in the early 2000s, Battle wasn't highly recruited. In fact, he wasn't recruited at all. After graduating from Mary Persons High in Forsyth, Georgia, in 2003, Tra Battle was handed his diploma without a single scholarship offer.

"Not from Furman, not from Georgia Southern," Battle said. "Nowhere."

So he chose Georgia for academic reasons. Still, Battle's dream to walk on brought him to Athens weeks before most scholarship players in the summer of 2003. And by August 30, 2003, he was one of two true freshman defensive backs traveling to the season-opener at Clemson. Thomas Flowers, the other freshman, ended up redshirting. Battle played.

"Winning the SEC title [in 2005] and getting those interceptions at Auburn in 2006 are both amazing memories," Battle said. "But nothing meant more than playing against Clemson. After no college offered out of high school, to play that first game of my freshman year meant everything."

DURING HIS FIRST THREE SEASONS IN ATHENS, Battle and the rest of Georgia's defense faced little adversity. From 2003 to 2005, UGA combined for a 31-8 record, two SEC championship game appearances, one conference title and multiple bowl wins. However, as 2006 wound down, Georgia was 6-4, its worst start since 1996. The Bulldogs had been upset by Vanderbilt and Kentucky. They'd also lost to Florida and Tennessee. Making it worse, it was Battle's senior year.

"Seasons like that aren't supposed to happen at Georgia," Battle said. "We're better than that. We came to Auburn with our pride at stake and a huge chip on our shoulder."

On the other hand, Auburn—quietly ranked No. 6 in the BCS standings—was on the verge of possibly winning its second SEC title in three years. The 2006 Tigers entered November 11 favored by two touchdowns and hadn't dropped a game since October 7. But Battle wasn't concerned about rankings. In the locker room before kickoff, as Pastor Troy secretly blared through his ears, Battle's only thoughts revolved around what slipped away a year before. "I was never more ready for any game in my life," Battle said. "I just had a feeling it was going to be special."

Battle intercepted Brandon Cox three times in the opening half, returning one for a touchdown, and he ignited Georgia to a 30–7 halftime lead. Battle caught more passes in the first half than every Tiger receiver combined. As a stunned home crowd looked on, Auburn's SEC and national title dreams had vanished in thirty minutes.

"The thing I remember most was Auburn's pregame ceremony," said Battle, who received an I.V. at halftime for the only time in his career. "They had Bo Jackson on the field and it was the last time they ever flew [War Eagle VI]. I can't describe how loud that stadium was before kickoff. But after the second quarter, I think we quieted the whole state east of Tuscaloosa."

In the game, Georgia outgained the Tigers 446 yards to 171 and outnumbered Auburn in offensive plays, sixty-six to thirty-seven. Cox, who battled a right knee injury, was intercepted four times and was just four of twelve for 35 yards. The victory marked Georgia's largest win over an Associated Press top-five opponent since beating Georgia Tech, 34–0, in 1942. The morning after the game, a headline in the *Atlanta Journal-Constitution* read, "Battle Wins This War."

Prior to facing UGA, Auburn's defense had allowed thirty points once in their last forty starts (2005 at Sanford Stadium). Unfortunately for the Tigers, Georgia could have eclipsed forty points if Richt hadn't respectfully kneeled the ball three times (at the Auburn seven-, ten- and twelve-yard lines) in the final two minutes. UGA turned the ball over on downs instead of further humiliating the home team.

YEARS HAVE COME AND GONE, but Battle still remembers that afternoon at Jordan-Hare Stadium. In his hometown of Forsyth, city administrators notarized November 11, 2006, as Tra Battle Day. For Father's Day in 2015, Battle was given two canvas prints. One depicts him preparing to lunge into Auburn's end zone. The second captures him fully extended over the goal line.

But no photograph compares to the joy he gets each autumn when he reminds his older sister, Taviana, an Auburn University graduate and nurse manager at Emory Healthcare in Atlanta, of what he did to her alma mater. Even during Battle's playing days, Taviana cheered for Auburn and wore orange and blue while sitting in the UGA family section.

"I'll never forget seeing [Taviana] after that game," Battle said. "Her face was absolutely priceless. But I have to give her credit—she still gave me a hug."

27

THE BLACKOUT—2007

GEORGIA 45, AUBURN 20

Lights were turned off as Georgia's team huddled together inside their locker room at Sanford Stadium. With heads bowed, players locked arms as kickoff against Auburn was minutes away.

"Before every home game," wide receiver Mikey Henderson said,

> *We had a team prayer where we'd all cram into the shower area just to get that feeling of togetherness. Imagine this: You have 100 guys crammed into a shower and we're saying the Lord's Prayer at the top of our lungs. It's completely black and feels like 1,000 degrees. But, look, for our team it gave us a sense of unity. That for the next four hours, it was about everyone in this room.*

After starting the 2007 season 4-2 and dropping to No. 24 in the Associated Press poll, UGA had started to gain momentum. On October 13, the Bulldogs beat Vanderbilt, 20–17. Georgia followed up with a 42–30 victory over defending national champion Florida on October 27 and, on November 3, defeated Troy, 44–34.

Then, in the week leading up to the Deep South's Oldest Rivalry, rumors swirled around Athens about the possibility of the team wearing black jerseys. The curiosity started when Mark Richt asked fans to blackout Sanford Stadium—but that's as far as he hinted. In reality, Georgia's senior class came up with the idea months earlier during a dinner at Richt's home in early August.

Above: Knowshon Moreno runs for a touchdown against the Tigers in 2007. *The* Augusta Chronicle.

Left: Members of Georgia's student section painted "Blackout" on their chests for the 2007 game against Auburn. *The* Augusta Chronicle.

"Every year, Coach Richt starts fall camp by inviting the senior class over," said Henderson, a senior in 2007. "While at his place, Coach Richt goes, 'Guys, what do y'all want out of this year?'"

The senior class delivered an uncommon request: a game in black. Richt didn't immediately commit to the idea, but said he'd consider the suggestion. About a week later, during a character-development meeting at fall camp, Richt again went to speak to the seniors, but this time with confirmation.

"No one else knew but the seniors," senior defensive back Kelin Johnson said. "We wanted it to be our secret."

The secret stayed hidden for nine weeks, until Richt demanded fans wear black to the Deep South's Oldest Rivalry. But even then, outside of Georgia's twenty-two seniors, no one truly knew what was happening. According to freshman Rennie Curran, students on campus wondered what the blackout entailed as hype escalated through the Classic City.

"Man, students were going crazy all week," said Curran, who turned nineteen the day of the game. "Everyone kept asking me if we were wearing black, but I had no idea. That's the truth. No one had a clue but the seniors and Coach Richt."

The afternoon of November 10, the Sanford Stadium bleachers were transformed into a sea of black, but Georgia fans had expectations tempered when players took part in pregame warm-ups wearing traditional red. Expectations further faded when team captains walked to midfield in red. Turns out, with nine weeks to perfect the blackout, UGA seniors had plotted multiple twists. With hopes of confusing fans and teammates, the seniors asked Richt if they could first wear red before making a last-minute change.

The request was met with initial resistance. With only minutes between warmups and kickoff, the task of putting on another jersey wasn't the issue. It was undoing tape, re-equipping linemen and getting every player ready to play. Eventually, however, Richt agreed to further confuse underclassmen.

"I was so disappointed when we got to the stadium," fullback Brannan Southerland said. "At that point, we all assumed we were wearing red."

Inside the locker room, however, a different story was unfolding. Following the team prayer, lights flipped on and black jerseys donned the back of each chair in Georgia's locker room.

"When I tell you we went crazy, I mean we went crazy," Curran said. "Everyone was tackling each other and next thing you know I get knocked to the ground by Trinton Sturdivant. Man, we would've beat any team in the country that night."

Mikey Henderson said, "I still get chills thinking back to that moment. Our whole locker room absolutely exploded."

Kelin Johnson remembered that "it was like Christmas morning."

On Auburn's first play, Johnson intercepted quarterback Brandon Cox, as UGA raced out to a 17–3 lead. But after surviving Georgia's onslaught, the Tigers rallied to take a 20–17 advantage midway through the third period. Then, as Henderson says, "Soulja Boy happened." With the popular song blaring throughout Sanford Stadium, Georgia's sideline began to dance. Much of the student section joined in. Eventually, CBS announcers Verne Lundquist and Gary Danielson even got in on the fun. From five minutes left in the third quarter to 6:48 remaining in the fourth, Georgia scored four touchdowns, turning a three-point deficit into a 45–20 rout. And with each score, "Soulja Boy" only seemed to get louder.

Defensive back Asher Allen looks over Auburn quarterback Brandon Cox. *Morris Communications.*

"No game embodied a sense of Georgia football, having fun and wearing the G like that night against Auburn," Henderson said. "It was the perfect storm."

Georgia finished 2007 by again wearing black in the Sugar Bowl. Facing an undefeated Hawaii team, UGA routed the Warriors, 41–10, en route to a No. 2 final national ranking.

Inside the Rivalry

Georgia's blackout wasn't the first jersey switch in the history of the Deep South's Oldest Rivalry. On November 18, 1978, Auburn coach Doug Barfield pulled the original locker-room swap. With Georgia needing a victory to clinch the SEC title, Auburn warmed up in blue jerseys before reentering the dressing room at Jordan-Hare Stadium. Inside, orange tops awaited.

"It was a very emotional reaction," Barfield said in 2016. "Responsive is probably the best word. We had to calm guys down before running out."

According to Auburn equipment manager Frank Cox, the idea was sparked after Notre Dame played arch-rival Southern California in 1977.

In a contest that later became known as the "Trojan Horse Game," Notre Dame warmed up in traditional blue jerseys before switching to Kelly green. The Irish, inspired by its new look, slaughtered USC, 49–19.

"Coach Barfield came to me that spring and said, 'You think we could ever do the same with orange?'" Cox recalled. "I said, 'Absolutely.'"

In the summer of 1978, Cox looked into the idea and eventually received an orange sample jersey with blue lettering. Afraid the dark numbers would prove difficult for fans to see, Cox walked into an empty Jordan-Hare Stadium and asked Auburn trainer Herb Waldrop to sit in the stands.

"No one else was there, so I went to the middle of the field and Waldrop went to the bleachers," Cox said. "Well, you couldn't read the number, so I took the jerseys back and they screen-printed white numbers over the navy. After we wore them against Georgia, there were lots of cracks in the white and you could see straight through to the blue. They looked a whole lot older than having been worn just once."

Auburn's equipment department received the orange jerseys before the 1978 season. Similar to UGA seniors in 2007, Cox, Waldrop and Barfield

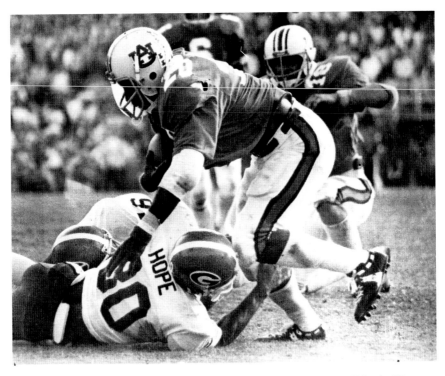

Auburn running back Joe Cribbs sports an orange jersey in 1978. *Auburn University Library Special Collections.*

kept quiet until November. "There wasn't any assurance we'd ever do it," Cox said.

But look, if Coach Barfield decided to, you couldn't just snap your fingers and get jerseys. So I ordered them that summer and they just sat in three boxes for months. I had no idea if I'd ever open them. Finally, during Georgia week, Coach Barfield was walking around practice and asks, "We still have those orange jerseys?" I said, "We sure do." He goes, "Let's try them and see what happens." That was the first time we had mentioned the orange jerseys since I ordered them, but I knew it was going to be a big deal.

How big of a deal? According to Cox, it was the most raucous he's ever seen a team before kickoff. "That locker room was up for grabs," said Cox, laughing.

Playing with something to prove, Auburn's offense tallied 502 yards (250 on the ground from Joe Cribbs), but four missed field goals by Jorge Portela proved to be the difference. Ultimately, the contest ended in a 22–22 tie, which still prevented Georgia from winning the conference title. "I call that game our 22–22 victory," Barfield said. "We ran up and down the field all day and I really believe we deserved to win."

Auburn out-rushed Georgia 438 yards to 93.

"Auburn's 1978 backfield was the best backfield in the history of college football," said UGA defensive back Scott Woerner. "I mean, Joe Cribbs, James Brooks, William Andrews. Auburn ran rampant on us."

Three controversial calls (two by officials, one by Vince Dooley) played large roles in the outcome. With 5:18 remaining, Willie McClendon scored on a one-yard run to bring UGA to within one point. However, instead of attempting a two-point conversion, Dooley had Rex Robinson kick the game-tying extra point. Dooley apologized to his team after the game for the decision. For Auburn, it was a story of inches. On the final play of the first half, fullback William Andrews broke loose for a forty-seven-yard run. However, as Andrews dove for the goal line, an official said his knee touched inches short (a call Andrews disagreed with). Finally, with 1:04 left in the game, Auburn faced fourth and inches from Georgia's thirty-three-yard line. Andrews again got the carry and surged forward for what seemed to be a first down. Officials thought otherwise. The ball was marked short of the line to gain, which prevented Auburn from keeping its drive alive.

"No question that was a first down," Barfield said. "We had a surge and I know [Andrews] made it."

Barfield's team again wore orange against Georgia in 1980 with hopes of upsetting the No. 1 Bulldogs. This time, the strategy proved unsuccessful. In what ended up being Barfield's final home game as Auburn's coach, the Tigers fell, 31–21, to the eventual national champions.

Auburn hasn't worn orange since.

"In 1981, Coach Dye came to me after he got hired," Cox recalled. "Dye tells me, 'I don't like orange,' so that was the end of that."

28

WE COMIN'—2010

AUBURN 49, GEORGIA 31

From ESPN to CBS, rumors swirled all week about allegations involving Cameron Newton and his father, Cecil. The news broke nationally on November 4, 2010, while the days leading up to the Deep South's Oldest Rivalry focused primarily on an alleged pay-for-play scandal rather than Auburn's 10-0 record. Were the claims true? Would Newton be in uniform? Was Auburn's undefeated season about to crumble inside Jordan-Hare Stadium?

The pregame focus may have been on allegations, but the eventual Heisman Trophy winner silenced his critics with two words: "We comin'." In his final home performance at Auburn, Newton shredded UGA to the tune of 151 rushing yards, 148 passing yards and four combined touchdowns. In a game dominated by outside noise, Newton's play was the most deafening.

FOR AUBURN AND GEORGIA FANS, the contest also marked the end of what many once considered a friendly rivalry. Georgia loyalists were largely outraged by the play of Auburn defensive tackle Nick Fairley, who flattened quarterback Aaron Murray on numerous occasions. Fairley was flagged for roughing the passer in the third quarter when he took two steps after Murray released a pass and drove his helmet into the quarterback's back. Fairley eventually knocked Murray out of the game with 2:01 remaining. When asked if his intentions were to injure Murray, Fairley said in 2015, "Of course not. We were in a war, a battle. I just go out there and do my job. You know, play between the white lines."

Philip Lutzenkirchen celebrates near UGA linebacker Alec Ogletree during the 2010 game in Auburn. *Morris Communications.*

UGA center Ben Jones backed up Fairley's statement: "He was playing hard. You get to the [National Football] League by getting sacks and hitting the quarterback and that's all he was trying to do. I've gotten to know Fairley since being in the NFL and he's a great guy. I have nothing bad to say about Nick Fairley."

Auburn fans were also upset, claiming UGA linemen had questionable blocks on Fairley throughout the contest. One play after Fairley's fourth-quarter hit sidelined Murray, Jones went after Auburn's All-American, which ignited a fight near Georgia's thirty-yard line. Michael Goggans was ejected for landing a punch on UGA's Clint Boling. According to Jones, a native of Centreville, Alabama, he was trying to exude protection for his injured quarterback.

"Me and Fairley were wrestling on the ground and we both looked up and no one's around," Jones said. "Everyone was fighting like ten yards away. We just looked at each other then walked over there side-by-side. We were like, 'Dang, we missed all the action.'"

Two plays later, another punch was thrown, resulting in Tiger lineman Mike Blanc getting ejected. Fairley and Jones shared similar reasoning behind the exchanges. Jones said: "I'm where I am today because I'm a competitor and play hard every snap. I'm not the most gifted athlete but I do have a nasty streak. When it comes down to it, I'm gonna do whatever it takes to win."

Fairley said: "Everyone's trying to get that 'W.' Yeah, things get chippy every now and then but I have nothing against Georgia. I know they have a great fan base and great players. It was never anything personal."

Still, between the late-game scuffles, Newton's allegations and the fact that Auburn eventually captured the BCS national title, November 13, 2010, changed how the Deep South's Oldest Rivalry feels to members of both fan bases.

THE GAME

The night before kickoff, Auburn tight end Philip Lutzenkirchen was exchanging text messages with UGA backup quarterback Hutson Mason. The two had been teammates at Lassiter High in Marietta, Georgia, and remained close until Lutzenkirchen's tragic death on June 29, 2014.

"Philip kept texting me about Cam Newton," Mason recalled. "He was saying how Cam was really aggravated about the allegations and that he was gonna take it out on us. Philip texted, 'Man, we're about to blow y'all out.'"

Nick Fairley (90) attempts to get to Georgia quarterback Aaron Murray. *John Kelley.*

Less than three minutes into the contest, Newton scored on a thirty-one-yard run to put Auburn in front, 7–0. But the Tigers' lead was short lived. Four minutes later, Georgia tied the contest when Aaron Murray found receiver A.J. Green. Later in the first quarter, Murray connected with fullback Shaun Chapas for a nine-yard touchdown. Suddenly, Auburn was down 14–7.

"We go up by seven and I look across the field at Philip," said Mason, laughing at the memory. "He gives me this little shoulder shrug."

With sixty seconds left in the opening quarter, Murray delivered another touchdown to Green, this time from forty yards, to put UGA ahead, 21–7. "We go up by fourteen and I lock eyes again with Philip from opposite sidelines," Mason said. "I start dying laughing and he's got this look like, 'Aw, man, what did I get myself into?' It was unique because he was rarely in that moment in life where you could prove him wrong, where you could one-up him."

Soon after, like so many times in 2010, Auburn roared back. The Tigers trailed 21–7 after fifteen minutes, but rallied to tie the contest going into halftime. Then, Auburn head coach Gene Chizik and special teams coordinator Jay Boulware elected to steal a possession from Georgia to open the third quarter.

"It's something we had practiced all season," said Wes Byrum, Auburn's placekicker. "Coach Boulware and Coach Chizik came up at halftime and said, 'Hey, we're gonna start the second half with this. Be ready to go.'"

The play? An onside kick, which Byrum squibbed to himself. Eleven yards later, Byrum hauled in the bouncing football and Auburn's offense was back on the field.

"We practiced that play all the time, so I had become very comfortable with it," Byrum said. "Still, it's hard because it wasn't something I could practice during the game. I mean, we can't show Georgia what we're about to do. You just hope you're ready and that it works in the moment."

Fortunately for Auburn, the execution was flawless. After taking over on its own forty-one-yard line, the Tigers drove fifty-nine yards in nine plays to take a 28–21 advantage. Onterio McCalebb capped the drive with a four-yard touchdown run. Byrum converted the extra point.

"It really got our momentum going," Byrum said of the onside kick. "And just as importantly, it took away a chance for Georgia to start the second half with anything positive."

THE PLAY THAT GAVE AUBURN A TWO-POSSESSION lead came with 8:05 left in the fourth quarter. Ahead 35–31, Newton found Lutzenkirchen

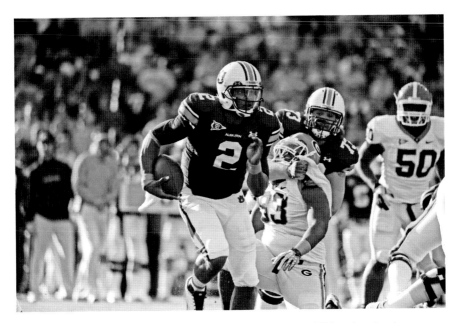

Heisman Trophy winner Cam Newton led Auburn to the 2010 SEC and national championships. *John Kelley.*

for a thirteen-yard touchdown to put the Tigers in front by eleven. It was Lutzenkirchen's second score of the game, marking his first multi-touchdown performance at Auburn. It was also the only game Mike Lutzenkirchen, Philip's father, ever missed. With Philip's grandmother battling cancer, Mike had flown to Illinois to be by her side, while his son helped clinch the SEC Western Division.

"I spoke with Philip on Saturday morning and he told me, 'Not sure how many times I'll be looked at in the passing game,'" Mike remembered. "It ended up being one of his most memorable games. I tell you what, we were all going crazy from Chicago."

Philip graduated from Lassiter High and had numerous classmates attend UGA. According to Mike, it was always the most anticipated game for his son. "He got up more for Georgia than any other opponent," Mike said of Philip, who passed away at twenty-three following a car accident in LaGrange, Georgia. "He had so many buddies that went to school in Athens, which made that rivalry extremely important to him."

One of Philip's closest friends was Mason. The two played together at Lassiter and Mason honored his fallen friend by having "43" stitched to his Georgia hat throughout his senior season in 2014. After graduating from

UGA, Mason married his high school sweetheart, Catherine McWalters, on June 26, 2015. Lutzenkirchen was listed as an honorary groomsman, while each of Mason's ten groomsmen wore "43" pins at the ceremony.

Mason reflected on Philip Lutzenkirchen with these words:

I spoke to Philip the night that he died. I was literally the last person to speak with him other than the people there that night. The other person who died in the car accident, Ian Davis, I also knew very well—he played baseball at UGA. We were exchanging text messages that night and I hadn't spoken with Philip in a month or so. He texted me out of the blue and asked how things were going. I said, "Spring ball went really well," and he said to me, "Even though I'm an Auburn man, you know I'll be rooting hard for you next season." We spoke a little more about the season and then shared a laughing joke about a Georgia player we both knew. That was it. He died that night.

Mason continued:

We were really, really close. I probably didn't tell him enough but I looked at him as an older brother. I have a younger brother, but I never had an older brother. Me and Philip were very close growing up—we played [youth] football together, middle school basketball, high school basketball and then obviously high school football at Lassiter. Growing up in East Cobb, everything Philip was doing I was doing, too. He was an awesome person. He was so funny, man. Besides my roommate in college [Brandon Burrows], Philip was the wittiest person I ever met in my life. There was nothing ever too awkward for him. If he met a fan at a burger joint, he'd turn it into a ten-minute conversation. He was special. Very, very special.

29

"BURN THE BULLDOG"

A LOST TRADITION AT AUBURN UNIVERSITY

David Housel can still feel heat from the bonfire.

For decades, Auburn students, marching band members and cheerleaders would hike the streets of campus for the annual "Burn the Bulldog" pep rally. The band led the parade, while students—many carrying homemade torches—followed close behind.

"Burn the Bulldog was probably the most eagerly anticipated event of fall quarter," said Housel, who graduated from Auburn University in 1969 and served as athletic director from 1994 to 2005. "But now, as they say in Georgia, it's gone with the wind."

Burn the Bulldog typically took place the Thursday night before Auburn faced UGA, while Housel estimates the bonfire lasted from the 1920s through late 1980s. Most sororities created handheld floats involving a bulldog, and fraternity members would carry the decorations through town. The parade traveled through campus and ultimately ended in the shadows of Auburn's football stadium. Awaiting the fans? A giant bonfire. One by one, floats would be viewed by parade judges before being thrown into the roaring flames.

"The parade was held after dark and it always seemed to be on a very cold Thursday night," said David Jackson, 1982 Auburn University graduate. "Of course, each float depicted a bulldog in various stages of distress, a warning so to speak, of the unfortunate outcome that was sure to come at the hands of our beloved Tigers."

Eventually, however, the bonfire was canceled due to safety reasons.

"Burn the Bulldog is gone because of lawyers and risk managers. Simple as that," Housel said. "As far as I'm concerned, it was the wrong decision. From a legal standpoint, OK, it was probably the right choice. But from a collegiate atmosphere perspective, it was terrible."

Around thirty handmade bulldogs were sacrificed each year, most of which contained a theme or slogan. In 1964, the winning float was a bulldog inside a hotdog bun boasting the name *Bun the Bulldog*. "It was the most fun night of the year," said Barbara Dooley, wife of Vince Dooley and 1960 Auburn graduate. "Looking back, it's amazing how naïve we were. We never thought about fire hazards or anything like that—all we did was throw bulldogs into the flames and yell, 'War Eagle.' I can't describe how wonderful of a tradition it was."

Dooley was a Delta Zeta and says her sorority made a float every year. The morning after the bonfire, most sororities would walk downtown to paint the windows of local businesses. "There were two Auburn events each fall that always stuck out in my mind," Dooley said. "Burn the Bulldogs was one and then we had 'Hey Day,' where you said hey to everyone you saw on campus. I had the best four years at Auburn. It really was like one big family."

For Housel, Burn the Bulldog went beyond a night of camaraderie. "That bonfire signaled the end of a regular week and meant Georgia was up next," Housel said. "When we played Georgia, something big was going to happen. Win, lose or draw, something very meaningful was going to take place."

Memories from the annual bonfire remain vivid for Housel and Dooley, who expressed disappointment that current students won't experience the same tradition. Still, for years after the bonfire was discontinued, Auburn had a parade to honor its final SEC home game of the season. In 1994, Auburn's Alpha Tau Omega fraternity made a float called "Auburn's Burning Da'Zeier" to taunt Georgia quarterback Eric Zeier. For an unknown reason, there was no parade in 1995, so, while running for president of the Student Government Association, Athens, Georgia native Tommy Bingham made a campaign promise to bring back a pep rally before the UGA game. Bingham won the election, and in 1996, Auburn held a celebration the Thursday of Georgia week. But no bulldogs were burned. There was no bonfire. And there hasn't been a bonfire for generations of Auburn students.

"If I said, 'Burn the Bulldog bonfire,' Auburn students today wouldn't know what I meant," Housel said. "That's a shame. That truly is a shame."

AFTERWORD

Before I left the homes of Vince Dooley and Pat Dye, the two coaches urged me to understand what makes the Deep South's Oldest Rivalry uniquely special. And it had nothing to do with each having spent time at both universities.

First of all, Dooley is 100 percent Bulldog. Dye is 100 percent Auburn. Neither attempted to hide their allegiance, and neither Dye nor Dooley regret where they've spent the better part of their adult lives. "I'm all Georgia," Dooley proudly stated.

"Auburn University is [one of] the best things that ever happened to me," Dye said.

While interviewing both coaches, I ended our time together with the same question: What makes the Auburn-Georgia game different? There was no right or wrong answer, but I still wanted opinions.

Surprisingly, their answers were almost identical.

"55-55-8," said Dye, referring to the series record during our September 2015 interview. "That's all you need to know."

Dooley said: "This rivalry began in 1892 at Piedmont Park. Now it's 2015 and the series is 55-55-8. All tied up. Try to find another game that's even after 118 meetings."

Georgia won the 2015 and 2016 contests, nudging ahead 57-55-8, its first lead in the series since 1986. Through 120 contests, thousands of players have come and gone. Coaches have changed. Stadiums have expanded. Still, as the second week of November approaches each fall, one game is guaranteed.

"The Deep South's Oldest Rivalry is as great of a rivalry as there is," Dooley said. "It's a proud rivalry. A family rivalry. Most of all, it's a respectful rivalry."

APPENDIX

LYNCH-YOUNG MEMORIAL TROPHY

Beginning in 1954, to honor UGA graduate Art Lynch and Auburn alumnus Alfred Young, the Lynch-Young Memorial Trophy was presented to the MVP of the Deep South's Oldest Rivalry.

Lynch and Young each resided in Columbus, Georgia, and played vital roles in keeping the contest there for more than four decades. Young was secretary of the Georgia-Auburn Football Association until his passing in 1953, while both men entertained many guests during game week. In 1953, Lynch and Young died within months of each other. Members of the Columbus Quarterback Club created the trophy on their behalf. The hardware was presented from 1954 until the game left Columbus in 1958. The award winners are as follows:

> *1954: Joe Childress (Auburn), Auburn 35, Georgia 0*
> *1955: Jerry Elliott (Auburn), Auburn 16, Georgia 13*
> *1956: Jimmy "Red" Phillips (Auburn), Auburn 20, Georgia 0*
> *1957: Jimmy Vickers (Georgia), Auburn 6, Georgia 0*
> *1958: Bobby Lauder (Auburn), Auburn 21, Georgia 6*

In honor of Art Lynch and Alfred Young, below is a list of deserving Lynch-Young Memorial Trophy recipients from 1959 through 2016.

2016: Georgia 13, Auburn 7
MAURICE SMITH. With UGA trailing 7–0, Smith intercepted Auburn's Sean White and returned it thirty-four yards for the game-tying score. Although Georgia's offense was held without a touchdown, the unranked Bulldogs stunned No. 9 Auburn, ending their dream of capturing the SEC title. The victory also marked Kirby Smart's first signature win at his alma mater.

Left: Jerry Elliott holds the Lynch-Young Memorial Trophy he won while playing for Auburn in 1955. *The Elliott family.*

Below: Jerry Elliott's original Lynch-Young Memorial Trophy he earned for helping Auburn beat Georgia in 1955. *The Elliott family.*

2015: Georgia 20, Auburn 13
ISAIAH MCKENZIE. Georgia's speedy sophomore broke free for a fifty-three-yard punt-return touchdown with 9:28 remaining in the fourth quarter. The play gave UGA a 56-55-8 edge in the all-time series, marking the Bulldogs first lead in the Deep South's Oldest Rivalry since 1986.

2014: Georgia 34, Auburn 7
NICK CHUBB. On nineteen carries, the UGA freshman ran for 144 yards and a pair of scores.

2013: Auburn 43, Georgia 38
NICK MARSHALL. Playing against his former school, Marshall ran for two touchdowns and threw for another, a seventy-three-yard game-winning heave to Ricardo Louis. The play became known as "The Prayer at Jordan-Hare."

Auburn would win the SEC title before falling to Florida State in the national championship game.

2012: Georgia 38, Auburn 0
AARON MURRAY. Statistically, Murray was the star, passing for 208 yards and three touchdowns. UGA's defense also made history, recording the first shutout for either team since 1976. Georgia would win the SEC East, but fell to Alabama, 32–28, in the conference title game.

2011: Georgia 45, Auburn 7
AARON MURRAY. Georgia's sophomore QB shredded Auburn's secondary for 224 yards, four touchdowns and no interceptions. UGA eventually lost to LSU, 42–10, in the SEC title game.

Freshman Nick Chubb tallied 144 yards on nineteen carries against the Tigers in 2014. *Morris Communications.*

2010: Auburn 49, Georgia 31
CAM NEWTON. Auburn's eventual Heisman Trophy winner combined for four touchdowns and 299 yards of total offense, propelling the Tigers to its first SEC West title since 2004. Auburn went on to win the Southeastern Conference and BCS national championship.

2009: Georgia 31, Auburn 24
CALEB KING. Despite having just ten carries, the UGA running back totaled sixty-six yards on the ground and two touchdowns.

2008: Georgia 17, Auburn 13
MATTHEW STAFFORD. It wasn't Stafford's prettiest offensive performance, but the quarterback did enough, throwing for 215 yards and two touchdowns.

Caleb King (4) scores one of his two touchdowns against Auburn in 2009. *Morris Communications.*

2007: Georgia 45, Auburn 20
KNOWSHON MORENO. Most remember Moreno's dance moves in a black jersey, but the New Jersey native also shined on the field with twenty-two carries for 101 yards and two scores.

2006: Georgia 37, Auburn 15
TRA BATTLE. Georgia's senior defensive back had three first-half interceptions, including one for a touchdown. Battle's performance eliminated No. 6 Auburn from SEC and BCS title contention. Georgia was unranked and thirteen-point underdogs.

2005: Auburn 31, Georgia 30
KENNY IRONS. The University of South Carolina transfer had thirty-seven carries for 179 yards and two scores. Irons, a Dacula, Georgia native also caught three passes for thirty-one yards. The year 2005 marked the first time since 1942 that Georgia lost to Auburn and still won an SEC title.

2004: Auburn 24, Georgia 6
RONNIE BROWN. Auburn's do-everything back led the Tigers in receiving yards (eighty-eight) while also rushing for fifty-one. Brown's thirty-four-yard touchdown catch extended Auburn's lead to 24–0 in the fourth quarter. Auburn finished the season 13-0, were crowned SEC champions and received national championship rings from head coach Tommy Tuberville. This was Auburn's first conference title since 1989 and first undefeated season since 1993.

2003: Georgia 26, Auburn 7
ODELL THURMAN. With Auburn's offense threatening early in the fourth quarter, Thurman, UGA's middle linebacker, picked off Jason Campbell and returned it ninety-nine yards for a touchdown. The win was UGA's first home victory over Auburn since 1991.

2002: Georgia 24, Auburn 21
MICHAEL JOHNSON. The Georgia receiver had only eleven receptions in 2002 coming into the Deep South's Oldest Rivalry, but against Auburn he tallied thirteen for 141 yards and the game-winning score. Johnson's TD propelled UGA to its first SEC championship since 1982.

2001: Auburn 24, Georgia 17
CADILLAC WILLIAMS. Auburn's true freshman tailback carried forty-one times for 167 yards and two scores.

2000: Auburn 29, Georgia 26 (OT)
BEN LEARD. In his final Auburn home game, the Hart County, Georgia native threw for two touchdowns and rushed for the game-winning score in overtime. Leard went 2-0 against Georgia as a starter. Auburn won the SEC West but fell to Florida 28–6 in the SEC championship game.

1999: Auburn 38, Georgia 21
RONNEY DANIELS. Auburn's wide receiver caught nine passes for 249 yards and two scores against the Bulldogs. In the second quarter alone, Daniels tallied five catches for 161 yards.

1998: Georgia 28, Auburn 17
OLANDIS GARY. UGA's running back rushed for 130 yards and two scores.

1997: Auburn 45, Georgia 34
DAMEYUNE CRAIG. The senior signal-caller led No. 16 Auburn to an upset in Athens over No. 7 UGA. Craig threw for 231 yards with three total

touchdowns (one passing, two rushing). Auburn would win the SEC West before falling 30–29 to Tennessee in the conference title game.

1996: Georgia 56, Auburn 49 (4 OT)
MIKE BOBO. After not starting the game, Georgia's quarterback threw for a career-high 360 yards, leading his unranked team to an improbable victory on the Plains. This was the first overtime contest ever played in the SEC.

1995: Auburn 37, Georgia 31
STEPHEN DAVIS. Davis scored a pair of first-quarter touchdowns, helping Auburn prevail in Athens. This was the final game at Sanford Stadium before the 1996 Olympics, which required the removal of Georgia's original hedges. At the end of the contest, many spectators removed a branch before leaving. It was also Ray Goff's final home game as Georgia head coach.

1994: Georgia 23, Auburn 23
JUAN DANIELS. Sure, the game ended 23–23, but there's no question this result meant more to Ray Goff's team. Trailing 23–9 late in the third quarter, UGA quarterback Eric Zeier connected with Daniels for a seventy-nine-yard score. UGA would snap Auburn's twenty-game win streak, marking the first time in Terry Bowden's tenure that he didn't leave the field victorious.

1993: Auburn 42, Georgia 28
JAMES BOSTIC. Auburn's running back scored three times (twice in the second quarter, once in the fourth), leading the Tigers to victory. Bostic rushed for 183 yards on nineteen carries, helping propel the Tigers to its first undefeated season (11-0) since 1958.

1992: Georgia 14, Auburn 10
RAY GOFF. In arguably his most memorable game as UGA head coach, Goff's team left Auburn fans stunned at Jordan-Hare Stadium. With nineteen seconds remaining, Auburn was on Georgia's one-yard line when the Tigers fumbled a handoff exchange. Watching the clock tick down, Goff motioned for his players to stay on the ground as the scoreboard eventually struck 0:00.

1991: Georgia 37, Auburn 27
GARRISON HEARST. Hearst was a workhorse for Georgia, totaling 115 rushing yards and a TD. The win was Georgia's first home victory over Auburn since clinching the SEC title at Sanford Stadium in 1981.

James Bostic (33) rushed for 183 yards on nineteen carries against the Bulldogs in 1993. *Morris Communications.*

1990: Auburn 33, Georgia 10

DENNIS WALLACE. On Georgia's opening possession, Wallace intercepted UGA quarterback Greg Talley, setting up the go-ahead score. Auburn's defense forced a pair of first-half turnovers to spark a 33–10 rout.

1989: Auburn 20, Georgia 3

REGGIE SLACK. Auburn's quarterback went nineteen of twenty-seven for 230 yards and a touchdown. The victory helped earn Pat Dye his fourth and final SEC crown.

Auburn quarterback Reggie Slack led the Tigers to a 1989 victory in Athens. *Morris Communications.*

1988: Auburn 20, Georgia 10
STACY DANLEY. Danley rushed for 172 yards, more than any back had gained against Georgia all season. The win secured Auburn its second straight conference championship.

1987: Auburn 27, Georgia 11
JEFF BURGER. Auburn's quarterback completed twenty-two of thirty-two passes for 217 yards and two TDs. The Tigers went on to clinch the SEC title.

1986: Georgia 20, Auburn 16
WAYNE JOHNSON. UGA's backup quarterback threw for a touchdown and rushed for another, leading his team to an upset over Auburn at Jordan-Hare. Georgia's starting QB, James Jackson, did not attend the game because of his grandmother's passing.

1985: Auburn 24, Georgia 10
BO JACKSON. Despite playing injured, the eventual Heisman Trophy winner rushed for two touchdowns—67 yards and 6 yards. In all, Jackson had nineteen carries for 121 yards. Jackson finished his career 3-1 in the Deep South's Oldest Rivalry.

Auburn running back Stacy Danley rushes for a first down against Georgia. *Morris Communications*.

1984: Auburn 21, Georgia 12
TOMMIE AGEE. Agee broke off a pair of long runs, helping Auburn race out to a 14–0 halftime advantage. This marked the first time Auburn had beaten UGA at Jordan-Hare Stadium since 1974.

1983: Auburn 13, Georgia 7
PAT DYE. The Auburn coach was carried off Sanford Stadium's field after beating his alma mater. The victory gave Dye his first SEC title, while also handing Georgia its first SEC defeat since 1979.

1982: Georgia 19, Auburn 14
HERSCHEL WALKER. Walker scored both Georgia touchdowns, rushing for 171 yards in his final game before the 1982 Heisman Trophy voting. Walker scored on runs of 47 and 3 yards.

1981: Georgia 24, Auburn 13
BUCK BELUE. Vince Dooley presented Belue with the game ball after UGA's senior quarterback threw touchdown passes of forty-six and five yards.

1980: Georgia 31, Auburn 21
GREG BELL. Trailing 7–3 in the second quarter, Georgia's Greg Bell blocked a punt, which was returned by Freddie Gilbert for the go-ahead score. UGA went on to win its first unanimous national title.

1979: Auburn 33, Georgia 13
JAMES BROOKS and JOE CRIBBS. The pair of Auburn backs combined for four touchdowns to end Georgia's Sugar Bowl dreams. Brooks amassed 200 yards against the Bulldogs, while Cribbs tacked on another 166.

1978: Auburn 22, Georgia 22
JOE CRIBBS. Auburn running back Joe Cribbs ran for 250 yards and a pair of TDs in the 22–22 tie. Cribbs scored on runs of 60 and 2 yards and added a 62-yard sprint. The tie prevented Georgia, who was unbeaten in the SEC, from winning the conference title.

1977: Auburn 33, Georgia 14
WILLIAM ANDREWS. Auburn's running back totaled 142 yards while scoring on carries of 1 and 32 yards.

1976: Georgia 28, Auburn 0
KEVIN McLEE. Georgia's tailback led the Dogs with 203 rushing yards on thirty carries en route to clinching Vince Dooley's third conference title. With quarterback Ray Goff unable to play due to an arm injury, UGA did not throw a pass the entire game but rushed for 470 yards.

1975: Georgia 28, Auburn 13
ALLAN LEAVITT. After Auburn was called for roughing the punter, Georgia kicker Allan Leavitt converted a fifty-one-yard field goal to put his team ahead, 21–13. Dooley called Leavitt's kick "The difference in the game." UGA would tack on an insurance touchdown to win, 28–13.

1974: Auburn 17, Georgia 13
PHIL GARGIS. Auburn's dual-threat quarterback rushed for more than one hundred yards, including the go-ahead touchdown.

1973: Georgia 28, Auburn 14
ANDY JOHNSON. The Athens native combined for three touchdowns (two rushing, one passing) to lift Georgia to a fourteen-point victory.

1972: Auburn 27, Georgia 10
KEN BERNICH. Auburn's sophomore linebacker intercepted a James Ray pass and returned it to Georgia's seven-yard line to set up the final score. Bernich's interception was one of six turnovers forced by the Tigers defense.

1971: Auburn 35, Georgia 20
PAT SULLIVAN. In a battle between two undefeated teams, Auburn quarterback Pat Sullivan proved to be the difference, throwing four touchdowns in Athens. The performance helped Sullivan capture the 1971 Heisman Trophy.

1970: Georgia 31, Auburn 17
JACK MONTGOMERY. With the game knotted at 17, Montgomery, a former quarterback, threw a fifty-two-yard halfback pass late in the third quarter. The trick play set up Georgia's game-winning touchdown. Entering the game, UGA was just 4-4, while No. 8 Auburn had Sugar Bowl dreams and a 7-1 record. Georgia's upset sent Auburn to the Gator Bowl.

1969: Auburn 16, Georgia 3
CONNIE FREDERICK. Frederick was on the receiving end of a twenty-four-yard touchdown from sophomore Pat Sullivan, which secured Auburn's victory.

1968: Georgia 17, Auburn 3
JAKE SCOTT. Georgia's defensive back had a pair of first-half interceptions, igniting UGA to a 17–3 halftime lead. Georgia scored all 17 points in the second quarter to earn Coach Vince Dooley his first outright SEC title.

1967: Georgia 17, Auburn 0
BILL STANFILL. Georgia's defensive lineman dominated the Tigers offense, helping limit Auburn to a mere eight total yards on the ground.

1966: Georgia 21, Auburn 13
VINCE DOOLEY. Auburn led 13–0 at halftime, but the Dogs rallied for twenty-one unanswered points to give Coach Dooley his first SEC crown—one he shared with Alabama. This was Dooley's first victory over mentor Ralph "Shug" Jordan. Dooley would go on to win five more SEC titles, all of which were clinched against his alma mater.

1965: Auburn 21, Georgia 19
TOM BRYAN and JOHN COCHRAN. Bryan, Auburn's junior fullback, rushed nineteen times for 162 yards, including a 41-yard touchdown in the first quarter. It was the first game that Bryan (a former quarterback) started at

fullback. Cochran played an equally large role in the victory. Cochran, an engineering student from Crossville, Alabama, forced a fumble, blocked an extra point and batted down a two-point conversion attempt.

1964: Auburn 14, Georgia 7
TUCKER FREDERICKSON. Frederickson rushed for 101 yards and a score. He alone topped Georgia's rushing output of 92 yards. Frederickson was named Player of the Year in the South in 1964 while finishing sixth in the Heisman Trophy voting. This marked Vince Dooley's first game against his mentor, Ralph Jordan.

1963: Auburn 14, Georgia 0
JIMMY SIDLE. Auburn's quarterback connected with halfback George Rose, of Brunswick, Georgia, for a fifty-five-yard scoring pass midway through the third period. The touchdown sealed the victory for the visiting Tigers. This was the last time Auburn shutout UGA.

1962: Georgia 30, Auburn 21
DON PORTERFIELD. Porterfield caught three touchdown passes (fifteen, thirteen and four yards) from quarterback Larry Rakestraw. Auburn entered the game 6-1, and many Bulldog fans view the upset as the biggest victory during the three-season era of head coach Johnny Griffith. UGA, which hadn't scored thirty points since beating Tulsa on October 29, 1960, limped into Cliff Hare Stadium with a 2-3-3 record. It left with an unlikely victory.

1961: Auburn 10, Georgia 7
WOODY WOODALL. With the game knotted at 7–7, Woodall, an Atlanta native, kicked a forty-nine-yard field goal (then an Auburn school record), lifting the Tigers to victory. The play gave Auburn their first win at Sanford Stadium.

1960: Auburn 9, Georgia 6
ED DYAS. Auburn's kicker connected on three field goals, helping the Tigers edge UGA at Cliff Hare Stadium. Dyas, who went on to be an orthopedic surgeon in Mobile, set an NCAA record with thirteen field goals in 1960. The game also marked Georgia's first trip to the Plains. UGA was the first of Auburn's traditional rivals (Alabama, Georgia, Georgia Tech and Tennessee) to agree to play at Cliff Hare Stadium.

1959: Georgia 14, Auburn 13
FRANCIS TARKENTON. With thirty seconds remaining, Tarkenton connected with Bill Herron on a fourth-down score to earn Georgia its first SEC title in eleven years. UGA fans stormed Sanford Stadium's field in celebration and climbed the goalposts. The win gave Wallace Butts his fourth and final conference crown.

SOURCES

This book began in 2011 with an off-the-cuff comment by University of Georgia swim coach Jack Bauerle. Five years later, it ended with an interview at the home of Hardy King, who caught the winning touchdown against Auburn in 1966.

In between King and Bauerle, hundreds of hours of research made this book a reality. However, it would not have been possible without cooperation from dozens of former players and coaches.

Vince Dooley welcomed me into his Athens home in the fall of 2015, as did Pat Dye. To be honest, the interview with Dye was meant to focus on his thirty-fifth anniversary of becoming head coach at Auburn University. But what I assumed would be a fifteen-minute interview for an *Augusta Chronicle* assignment evolved into three and a half hours of riding on a golf cart and digesting seven decades of football memories.

Special thanks needs to be given to employees at the Auburn University Special Collections Library, who provided countless boxes of historical documents for me to sort through.

UGA alumni interviewed for the book (by e-mail, telephone or in person) were the following (the year given indicates the chapter the person is primarily featured in): Pat Dye, Don Leebern, Riley Gunnels (Memorial Stadium), Jack Bauerle (1971), Loran Smith (1959), Charley Britt (1957 and 1959), Don Soberdash (1959), Jon Stinchcomb (2002), David Greene (2002), Damien Gary (2002), Kevin Breedlove (2002), Dennis Roland (2002), Ken Veal (2002), John Lastinger (1982 and 1983), Nat Dye (1957), Jimmy Orr

(1957), Sonny Seiler (1968, 1986 and 1996), Wayne Johnson (1986), Steve Boswell (1986), Mike Bobo (1996), Matt Stinchcomb (1996), Corey Allen (1996), Ronnie Jenkins (1965), Kirby Moore (1966), Hardy King (1966), Mike Cavan (1968), Bill Stanfill (1968), Ken Shaw (1968), Scott Woerner (1980), Frank Ros (1980), Rex Robinson (1980), Greg Bell (1980), Mitch Davis (1992), Ray Goff (1992), Juan Daniels (1994), Eric Zeier (1994), Hugh Nall (1999), Reggie Brown (2004), Fred Gibson (2004), Tra Battle (2006), Mikey Henderson (2007), Kelin Johnson (2007), Brannan Southerland (2007), Rennie Curran (2007), Ben Jones (2010) and Hutson Mason (2010).

Auburn alumni interviewed: Vince Dooley, Tim Christian, Dick Copas, Tucker Frederickson, Jerry Elliott (Lynch-Young Memorial Trophy), Barbara Dooley (Burn the Bulldog), David Housel (Burn the Bulldog), David Jackson (Burn the Bulldog), Roger Mitchell (1971), Terry Henley (1971), Dick Schmalz (1971), Tommy Yearout (1971), Bryant Harvard (1959), Jackie Burkett (1957 and 1959), Nick Marshall (2013), Ricardo Louis (2013), Randy Campbell (1983), Lloyd Nix (1957), Tim Baker (1957), Jeff Burger (1986 and 1987), Brent Fullwood (1986), Tom Bryan (1965), John Cochran (1965), James Brooks (1980), Alexander Wright (1987), Stan White (1992), Jim Voss (1992), Matt Hawkins (1994), Ben Leard (1999), Ronney Daniels (1999), Junior Rosegreen (2004), Courtney Taylor (2006), Karibi Dede (2006), Nick Fairley (2010) and Wes Byrum (2010).

In addition to interviews, numerous historical articles were used as information, including archives from the *Augusta Chronicle*, *Athens Banner-Herald*, *Columbus Ledger*, *Columbus Enquirer*, *Columbus Ledger-Enquirer*, *Atlanta Journal*, *Atlanta Constitution*, *Atlanta Journal-Constitution*, *Macon Telegraph*, *Opelika-Auburn News*, *Montgomery Advertiser* and *Birmingham News*. Microfilm articles from Georgia newspapers can be found at the main library at the University of Georgia. Microfilm from Alabama newspapers were viewed at the Auburn University library.

A handful of books were also used in this book, including: *No Ifs, No Ands, A Lot of Butts: 21 Years of Georgia Football*, co-written by Ed Thilenius and Jim Koger; *Dooley: My 40 Years at Georgia*, written by Vince Dooley with Tony Barnhart; *History of the University of Georgia* by Thomas Walter Reed; *Lost in the Lights: Sports, Dreams, and Life* by Paul Hemphill; *Dooley's Playbook: The 34 Most Memorable Plays in Georgia Football History*, written by Vince Dooley and illustrated by Steve Penley.

INDEX

ABOUT THE AUTHOR

Doug Stutsman is a native of Athens, Georgia, but attended high school and college in Macon.

Doug graduated from Tattnall Square Academy in 2003 and received a finance degree from Mercer University in 2007. Ultimately, his love for sports won out, and he's covered an array of subjects for the *Augusta Chronicle* since 2013.

Though raised by Auburn University graduates, he was never able to suppress his curiosity for UGA traditions and ultimately spent years researching his first book on the Deep South's Oldest Rivalry.

Regardless of the colors you don, come the second week of November, no one can deny the rich history of a contest woven through three centuries of competition.